T0153029

DONALD CULROSS PEATTIE LIBRARY
PUBLISHED BY TRINITY UNIVERSITY PRESS

An Almanac for Moderns

A Book of Hours

Cargoes and Harvests

Diversions of the Field

Flowering Earth

A Gathering of Birds:
An Anthology of the Best Ornithological Prose

Green Laurels:
The Lives and Achievements of the Great Naturalists

A Natural History of North American Trees

The Road of a Naturalist

WITH ILLUSTRATIONS
BY HENRY B. KANE

Diversions of the Field

DONALD CULROSS PEATTIE

TRINITY UNIVERSITY PRESS
San Antonio, Texas

Published by Trinity University Press
San Antonio, Texas 78212

Originally published as *Sportsman's Country*

Copyright © 2013 by the Estate of Donald Culross Peattie
Copyright © 1949, 1950, 1951, and 1952 by Donald Culross Peattie
Illustrations copyright © 1952 by Henry B. Kane

ISBN 978-1-59534-170-9 (paper)
ISBN 978-1-59534-171-6 (ebook)

All rights reserved. No part of this book may be reproduced in any form or by any electronic or mechanical means, including information storage and retrieval systems, without permission in writing from the publisher.

Trinity University Press strives to produce its books using methods and materials in an environmentally sensitive manner. We favor working with manufacturers that practice sustainable management of all natural resources, produce paper using recycled stock, and manage forests with the best possible practices for people, biodiversity, and sustainability. The press is a member of the Green Press Initiative, a nonprofit program dedicated to supporting publishers in their efforts to reduce their impacts on endangered forests, climate change, and forest-dependent communities.

The paper used in this publication meets the minimum requirements of the American National Standard for Information Sciences—Permanence of Paper for Printed Library Materials, ANSI 39.48-1992.

Cover design by BookMatters, Berkeley
Cover illustration: maikid/istockphoto.com

CIP data on file at the Library of Congress.

17 16 15 14 13 | 5 4 3 2 1

FOREWORD

AMERICAN NATURE, only three centuries ago a continent of wilderness, has become the cherished preserve of our people, under benevolent law. Before the hunter shoulders his gun or the rodsman his creel, he must first betake himself to get a license for his sport. So, too, when the naturalist sets forth into such terrain as is proclaimed in the title for these pages, he may well be asked to stop and show his credentials.

Mine I obtain on the authority of the big dictionary that opens so weightily on its stand at my window to deliver its verdicts. "Sport," it declares, "is a diversion of the field." By this definition, surely, the naturalist is a sportsman of a sort, innocent, perhaps in many ways ignorant. Though I have never shot at anything but tin cans, and am a fisherman scarcely more proficient, yet I venture that even those happiest with rod or rifle are no happier than I in my own "diversions of the field." Nor do I return home at the day's end empty-handed. This dozen of chapters is my kind of bag.

They are offered to my fellow sportsmen with humble admiration for their own wood-wisdom, their own seasoned knowledge of trout pool or quail covert. A conservationist to the core, I have no quarrel with any law-abiding hunter or fisherman. The best of them are shrewd naturalists themselves, from whom I can learn much. Certainly here I have no thought of teaching them anything of the sports in which I am not even a beginner, yet it is for them these chapters were written, at the invitation of Mr. Ted Kesting, editor of the magazine *Sports Afield*, whom I thank heartily for his cordial permission to make of them this little volume.

Perhaps their own diversions may gain a little from a glance at mine. That, in these chapters, has been to sport a little with the solemn-sounding subject of ecology, or bionomics. Ecology, pronounces the ponderous fat judge established at my window, is "the branch of biology which deals with the mutual relations between organisms and their environment." That's to say, of course, that it deals with the jack rabbit and the desert he jumps in, the bobwhite and the weed fields he feeds in, the mule deer and the forest he hides in. So have I done, and if you see sometimes more of the scene than the creature that dwells there, so I meant you to do. The hunter I can trust to keep his eye out for the game, the fisherman his gaze on his line. But in Nature each living thing, cattail or marsh bird, gray squirrel or hickory tree, is as important as any other. Each is interdependent on others, in that grand brotherhood. Only when it is killed can the animal be withdrawn from its environment and exhibited in solitary splendor.

This bag of a dozen still keeps, I hope, some breath of life in each trophy. So you must take them as they are, still free and elusive, still involved with the plants or creatures on which they feed, the woods or waters that are home to them. There, as long as the game laws hold and men obey them, as long as the woods stay green and the fence rows keep their covert, these creatures loved of hunter and naturalist alike will boldly pursue their own best sport — the dangerous game of life in the wild. And we shall both of us go afield to find them, and meet there in fellowship, as in this little book.

DONALD CULROSS PEATTIE

CONTENTS

Bobwhite Country	**1**
Gray Squirrel Country	15
Trout Country	29
Jack Rabbit Country	43
Valley Quail Country	59
Woodchuck Country	75
White-Winged Dove Country	91
Bass Country	107
Mule Deer Country	123
Red Fox Country	139
Hawk Country	153
Marsh Country	167

BOBWHITE COUNTRY

You can talk about your booming prairie chickens or your wild turkey (when you can find him!) or those welcome immigrants, the ring-necked pheasant and Hungarian partridge; and admittedly the ruffed grouse is a king of the tall timber. But the sweetest upland game bird in the eastern half of our country — perhaps in all the world — is the common bobwhite. They call him, not too accurately, a quail in New England, and down south he is a partridge, which is, ornithologically, a little closer to the facts. But why not accept the bird's

own name for himself, as he sits on the old snakerail fence in the May dusk, calling and calling?

"Bob-WHITE! Bob-bob-WHITE! Ah, Bob-White!"

And that is best, for Bob is not quite a true partridge nor a true quail; he is just himself, the best-known member of the White family, loved by sportsman and ornithologist alike, by the man of eighty autumns and the child learning his first birds. He is loved for what, uniquely, he is — for his confiding ways, for the thrilling explosion of the "quail bomb" and the matchless sport it provides. But, like most birds, like our deer and bears and foxes, like the very wild flowers, he is loved, too, for the kind of country he inhabits, for his natural setting.

That setting is so familiar to Americans living east of the Appalachians, or in them, that many of them accept as natural all that actually makes it unique — and makes it good for bobwhites. For this species, which is rightly the most all-around popular game bird of the uplands, is not an inhabitant of inaccessible peaks, like ptarmigan, or far off plains, like the sage hen, or demanding of virgin environment, like the prairie chicken. Bobwhite delights in — indeed he depends on for his increase — simple familiar features of the American landscape, farm and field, wood lot and fence row. The old-fashioned element in our American scene is actually essential to quail maintenance. I mean the one-mule farms, the small abandoned fields coming up to broomsedge grass. I mean the old snake-rail fences and the fence-row thickets of sassafras and sumac. I mean a land where clean agriculture is not practised, where the wild is never far off and always ready to press softly back.

That's bobwhite country. It is log cabin country too, and whippoorwill and firefly country, sunbonnet and barefoot country, and the country of the 'possum and the 'simmon tree, of butternuts and bee-gums and buttermilk in crocks on rock shelves in the old cold spring-houses. I spent much of my childhood in bobwhite country, then left it for more illustrious places, more crowded years — New England college years, New York City and Riviera years, and now I live in southern California. But I get hungry for that first, that simple country America, and I want my sons to know it, as part of their birthright.

That's why I have brought each of them all the way across the continent, as soon as he reached fifteen, to let them know for themselves the soft country roads that squirm like angleworms, the autumns blazing with the colors of huckleberry leaves and blackberries, poison ivy and Virginia creeper. I let them find for themselves the trout pools at the foot of old beeches, and feel on their skins the languor of Indian summer noons, and learn how to drink spring water — on the belly, with face in the crystal and the cress.

And sooner or later some old bachelor bobwhite, still

hopeful in his single unblessedness, would mount a fence post, and flinging up his head and tail together, would set the sky to ringing with his *bob-bob-white!* And the boy would turn to me with a smile of pure delight, as if an old legend, only half believed back in California, had come true.

If we were lucky, the boy and I, we might hear the "whisper call" of our friend Bob, given when danger is nigh, but not so near as to dictate retreat; it's like the cheery *bob-bob-white!* but so soft it carries only a few yards. Sooner or later, if we listened long enough and knew what to listen for, we detected the caterwauling note that Negroes transliterate as "walks dis way, walks dis way." Ornithologists say it is used for bluffing other males. Some of the scientists believe no other creature save man has so vast a vocabulary — that is, a meaningful vocabulary; I exclude the imitative powers of catbirds, parrots and mynas, and the gobbledygook of crows. Students of the bobwhite list such phrases as the following: the food call given by the cock bird when bringing home the bacon; the screaming battle cry of the cock when another male takes too much interest in his mate; the flicker-like cackle of the male in pursuit of his love affairs; the note of the hen that invites the male; and a great deal of baby talk. That is to say, the various notes of the chicks — the metallic piping of the lost chick, the childish chatter of youngsters keeping in touch with each other while feeding in the grass, and the curlew-like wail of the captured chick, a sound that brings down upon your head, your face, your very eyes, a demon in feathers — the parent bird.

All this is but a fraction of bobwhite language, yet the sweetest note of the lot I have not mentioned. It is that liquid, far-ringing *ka-lo-ee-hee* that sounds like some Polynesian song of welcome. Ornithologists call it the scatter call, meaning that it calls the scattered flock together. I would rather call it the all-clear signal, given when danger is past. It is also the bobwhites' version of "Oh, what a beautiful morning!" For with it they salute the dawn. Covey answering covey on a spring dawn, the sound goes on to the auditory horizon and presumably beyond it, and beyond the beyond, to the dewy rim of morning.

If the terrain is ideal for bobwhite, it has three or four features in combination, and in each of these environments the quail may spend a part of his life and a part of his day. First of all, there is the beloved fence-row thicket or the edge of the wood lot. These furnish him with sanctuary, but not less importantly, this is the best year-around dining room of the covey. Blackberries, dewberries, huckleberries, mulberries, and strawberries are spread here by the generous hand of Nature. And here the holly, cherry, wild rose, wax myrtle, sassafras, sumac, juniper and dogwood drop their succulent fruits. Pine seeds are an even greater favorite with all ages of bobwhite, and acorns too, though quail don't take to a dense thicket of scrub oak any more than they do to wet swampy woods, or deep tall timber where the dew lasts too long.

Yet dew is their favorite drink, and they get it abundantly in the fields of broomsedge grass. Broomsedge, known also as bluestem and Indian beard grass, is the second most important habitat of bobwhite, and probably every hunter knows it well by sight if not by name. Knee high to hip high, invading abandoned fields in about their third or fourth year and holding the ground till the pines begin to take over, broomsedge in the hunting season is russet or tawny, and has opened its big branched clusters of seeds to show the web of gray hairs that has given it the alternative name of beard grass. Although Bob does not eat its seeds, more than half of all bobwhite nests, in one intensively studied area, were found in broomsedge, and only sixteen per cent in woodland. Broomsedge leaves and old, bronzed pine needles are the favorite nesting materials — proving the old adage that the best place to hide a stone is on the beach.

The fallowed field, and the stubble after a grain crop, make up the third favorite hunting ground. Here is where Mr. Robert White proves himself the farmer's friend by devouring potato and striped cucumber beetles, squash lady birds, cinch bugs, clover weevils, bollworms, locusts and grasshoppers. While gleaning the ground carefully for small grains in the stubble, he pecks up untold quantities of weed seeds — ragweed and beggartick and witch grass, bindweed and morning glory, smartweed and crane's-bills.

Bobwhite country that is actually being managed in favor of quail breeding provides the fourth and best setting. Here crops are planted in the birds' interests, the legumes for the seeds of which quail have a passion. In the woods, they eat such wild legumes as the groundnut's tubers, the seeds of the wild bean and the hog peanut. In the open, they go for butterfly pea and that yellow-flowering, sensitive-leaved cassia named, in their honor, the partridge pea. So quail farmers plant vetch and Austrian winter pea, soybeans, Japan clover, and cowpeas, and such natives as the tick trefoils and bush clovers. There is no doubting or denying that, in any country, quail abundance shows a directly proportionate relation to the abundance of legumes, wild or cultivated. By comparison, control of snakes and hawks and all the other predators of the bobwhite is unimportant. A district that is supposed to be shot-out is much more likely to be deficient in legumes. And the preserve where no gun is allowed to sound may still be empty of quail if barren of his food.

Primarily, of course, Bob's country is close to the ground. There he eats and nests and hides. He is a ground bird. It is so natural to think of birds in terms of flight, whether we mean the mighty travel of ducks, or the soaring of a hawk, or the fluttering drive of migrating warblers, that a ground bird, such as all quails are, is almost a contradiction in terms, like a grounded aviator. When a bird gives up flight as its principal reliance for escape, it gives up — so it would seem — the chief advantage of being a bird. It has, literally, come down in the world. It sinks to the ecological level of snakes, skunks, weasels, foxes, curs, homeless cats, pot-hunters, and other earth-bound predators. Each of these would seem to be faster, or stealthier, more numerous, or more intelligent than the little bobwhite who so confidingly lets you know, at the top of his syrinx, just where he is. Who builds his nest close to trails and roadsides, and right on the ground where any night prowler can reach it. A creature with scarcely more means of defense than the cottontail, and not half a rabbit's spawning ability. A creature so fanatically parental that it will stick to the eggs even when cattle and horses are trampling the grass all about it, or bird dogs flairing within two feet of it. Even when a human hand is extended before the bird's very eyes (especially if the cock happens to be incubating while the hen is off), the unflinching parent will peck at the threat with fury.

Yet though life seems so precarious for this little groundling, it is doubtful if a shearwater is better adapted to life at sea, or a swift to the upper atmosphere, than the bobwhite to life among the fallen leaves. He *can*

fly — no sportsman needs to be told that; he can even
fly fast; in the first burst of speed a quail may be going
thirty-five miles an hour. But the odd, whirring, rather
mechanical flight always breaks up soon into a long,
low glide. In the glide the bird shows a bat-like skill
in avoiding obstacles, and great strategy and control in
seeming not to be heading for cover but passing it and
then, at the last second, veering into it with the maneu-
verability of a jet fighter.

This is merely to make the best of poor flight-power.
And Bob's forte is not even in his trick of running on
the ground and dodging, like a quarterback going
through an eleven united to stop him. The capacity
that makes this defenseless, tasty morsel, for which
dozens of natural enemies hunger, somewhat triumphantly safe is the disappearing act. Many birds and
quadrupeds have the power to "freeze." You see cottontails trying it vainly, and bitterns with incredible
success. But a motionless quail on the ground, especially on the woodland floor, is unsurpassed for invisi-
bility. Perhaps others are keener-eyed than I, but I
confess I can count on my fingers all the times I have
ever seen a quail covey on the forest floor — I mean,
before I accidentally stumbled on what I took to be a
heap of sun-and-shade-dappled leaves — and drove it
up. In no case, of course, have I seen the covey before
it saw me, for, with each bird's tail pointing inward,
each head gazing outward, the covey — you might say

— as one organism, is looking in every direction. More, bobwhites, being ground birds, appear to be especially sensitive to footfalls. If they can sense the approach of Reynard the light-footed, as some say they can, you or I must sound to them like a stone colossus on the march. If they keep their place even at our near approach, it is because they know that the most strategic advantage of their famous "bomb" is the element of surprise.

A veteran hunter, from the behavior of a well-trained dog, knows just about when he is going to get his shot at a covey, and is so cool of nerve and eye and hand that he drops his bird in those few seconds between the time the bomb explodes and the moment when the scattered fragments drop into cover. I must confess that the concussion of the explosion gives me, each time, a big jump. The feathered gyroscopes, some of them seeming to come right for my head, have me as baffled as the whirring sound — with a whistle or whine in it — that comes from every side. And before I could say "Why, it's quail!" I'd be too late for a shot if I went armed, which I don't. In fact, before Nimrod himself could pronounce *"Colinus virginianus virginianus* (Linnaeus)" — his chance would be gone. Already from the cover the old birds will be rapping out that mechanical message in code: *to-il-ick-kick-kick,* over and over, to which the chicks are absolutely responsive. For it means that horrible danger is right at hand. The birds, too, are right at hand — that's the baffling part of this king of all ground birds. You hear them all about you, the alarm cry spattering like hail on a tin roof, but not a feather can you see. Only the hunting dog can put even one of the birds to flight — by following the scent, as we cannot do, right to its source.

And even with his scent Bob can be sly. Not that he can control it as a man can put out a cigarette if he does not wish it smelled or seen. But the net results of smart quail behavior amount to much the same thing. A quail moving about, or preening, scratching or foraging, feeding or courting his mate, has a strong odor — not even agreeable when the human nose can detect it. Frightened, scattered, or fleeing birds all send forth a bold scent. But a covey that has been resting some time with closed wings has no odor — to judge from the behavior of bird dogs. A hen bird that has been incubating her eggs, without moving, for several hours is all but invisible, all but unsmellable, all but unflushable (if there are such words).

Loving his own country so much, Robert White, Esquire, is no great traveler, and tales of bobwhite migrations are based (when based on facts at all) on the purely local movement of these birds when driven out by population pressure, or tractors, fires, or floods, to some new ground. By inclination the quail doesn't travel a mile from his birthplace. Like most contented

people, he makes a fine husband and father. Once
mated, Bob is too sensible to double trouble, and remains monogamous for the season, perhaps sometimes
for life. Frequently he builds the nest, and occasionally
does all the incubating, especially if his mate dies. Old
bachelor Bobs can easily be persuaded to adopt chicks,
and father birds, like the human fathers who have the
most children, will always make room for a stray child.
Even when his wife does the incubating, Bob generally baby-sits for an hour or so in the afternoon, while
she gets a little recreation.

For quail — sensible birds — spend a great deal of
time enjoying their families and talking together, or
taking family dust baths in the dry lee of some old log,
or preening their feathers, or just plain loafing around.
They seem to do a lot of that on Indian summer noons
— and who's to blame them? At twilight they start for
the family or neighborhood roost, coming in from every
direction on long easy glides, or they walk home
quietly, like people who let themselves in by the back
gate. If they are still a few minutes early, they make
no attempt to utilize their time in a busybody way,
but stand quietly about together in the gathering dusk,
waiting for shut-eye.

The last time I heard a bobwhite calling it was almost dusk in a place called Happy Valley. I had heard
a lot of fine birds that day, in that place; I had started
up some ruffed grouse in the woods, and listened to

the madcap chatter of the chat, and imitated him and answered back till my cheeks were sore; I had heard and seen a tanager — always a red-feathered day in my diary — and had met some of the Happy Valleyites who seemed as contented as they should be. Southern summer was fast coming on in late May; I was glad when even so good a day gentled toward a cool close. Then, just as a bat let himself drop on an eddy of midges from the twinkling point of the evening star, I heard for the last time that year, the *bob-bob-WHITE!* of a solitary bird. It was more than what the animal behaviorists insist bird song is — a proclamation of territory. At least, it meant more to me. It meant that there were still Happy Valleys left. That in this troubled world something aboriginal and simply American is undeparted, and will last, I reckon, about as long as the hickories hold out and crickets sing in the broomsedge and the lean boys with husky voices go courting with their long-barreled guns and their dogs about them. When these things are changed, if they ever are, bobwhite country will be all changed too. And its best spokesman, surely, will not be there either.

GRAY SQUIRREL

COUNTRY

It was only a bunch of raw recruits, scared farm boys, that an officer discovered cowering in the shelter of a bank, that day at Shiloh. When a gray whirlwind letting out the Rebel yell had charged, they hadn't seemed to know how to use their rifles. But their officer, from their home state, understood them. "Next time," he told them, "just pick out a man, pretend he's a gray squirrel, and bring him down off the tree."

The boys from the hickory groves grinned. With their line reformed behind no more shelter than a snakerail fence, they did such execution that day that their position won the battle-given name of "the hornets' nest." Yet there seem to have been plenty of squirrel hunters in gray uniforms too. For the rattle of musketry at Shiloh rose to one continuous roar, veterans remembered, that never ceased till each side had suffered ten thousand casualties — one fourth the forces engaged. From the days of the first pioneers, the sure aim of such squirrel hunters has made the American a sharpshooter without peer.

Why call them squirrel hunters, you ask? Weren't they equally deer hunters or bear hunters? The answer is that one shot a week would supply a pioneer family with meat from such big game, but the wily, sidling, bounding, abundant squirrels gave, and required, continual expert rifle practice. Men who hunted them could shoot out the flame of a candle six times in succession without the lead's touching the wax. They could bark a squirrel off a tree without grazing a hair of its fur.

"The gun was wiped," wrote John James Audubon, explaining how this was done by the eighty-year-old Daniel Boone, "the powder measured, the ball patched with six hundred-thread linen, and the charge sent home with a hickory rod. We moved not a step from the place, for the squirrels were so numerous it was unnecessary to go after them. Boone pointed to one of these animals which was crouched on a tree and bade me mark well the spot which he intended to hit. The whip-like report resounded through the woods and along the hills, in repeated echoes. Judge of my surprise when I perceived that the ball had hit the piece of bark immediately beneath the squirrel and shivered it into splinters, the concussion produced by which had killed the animal, and sent it whirling through the air as if it had been blown up by the explosion of a powder magazine."

In Boone's day there were squirrels aplenty, even with such markmanship against them. A single hunting party in pioneer times in Michigan killed twenty thousand squirrels in a week. In 1794 Pennsylvania placed a price of threepence on each squirrel's head, and paid out in one year eight thousand pounds sterling for six hundred and forty thousand of the little cornpatch thieves. But something over a century later, five men in two days of hunting were able to take but three squirrels — and wrote up their luck and prowess for a sporting magazine! Their pitiful bag came out of "the best gray squirrel country" in West Virginia.

Gray squirrel country — what a host of home-like, Currier and Ives pictures come to mind at the very words! For gray squirrel country is primeval hardwood forest. It is — or it was — the America that Audubon painted, when the unbroken forests of beech nourished with their mast the passenger pigeons in sun-darkening hosts. Then the wood duck, now so rare, nested in the trees by every forest stream. Then the elk clashed antlers in male combat, where now the tractor lumbers around to charge at its own dust. And in places where today are clamorous, reeking cities, the lordly racket of the pileated woodpecker was the loudest sound, and there was no smoke but the haze of the Indians' hunting fires. Still today, wherever you can find it, gray squirrel country is a bit of early America, as native as a coonskin cap, as maple sugar on your flapjacks, or a black walnut cradle.

The sportsman, when he thinks of this environment, thinks too of the fine game animals that share it with the gray squirrel. He remembers the whistling flight of the woodcock, he recalls the Virginian deer, a velvet-eyed doe, perhaps, with her speckled fawn standing, frozen, close to her flank, his body blending with mottled light and shade of the leafy mansion they inhabit. He thinks of the ruffed grouse drumming on the forest floor. Of those woods flaming with autumn colors, the gold and scarlet leaves drifting down, in the frosty air, around him and his dog. Of the white page of winter, and the writing on it — footprints of deer mice and weasel, and the telltale spot in the snow where a gray squirrel came down to unearth his nut cache, and the clumped tracks of his frantic dash for the nearest tree when some stealthy fox discovered him.

This environment the naturalist calls the mesic deciduous forest — mesic being scientific shorthand for "middle of the road." That is, it goes to no extremes (or only passing excesses) of heat or cold, of wetness or dryness. In summer its filmy leaves shut out the heat but not the emerald light that filters to the forest floor. They lay the dust, keep in the dew, temper the wind. Then in winter when all the light and warmth available are needed, the leaves are gone. So the snow

never lingers long as it does under evergreens. Severe
though the winter, spring comes early; the black forest
loam absorbs the heat under the still leafless trees, and
a carpet of early wild flowers — spring-beauties, hepat-
icas, trout lilies, and Dutchman's breeches — springs
swiftly up. The trees here are some of our noblest —
beech and oak and ash and maple — and the whole setting is American Nature at its most livable and lovable.

The gray squirrel has the same high opinion of it
that we have. He is conscious, even if he cannot count
them, of the more than two hundred and fifty species
of trees that compose the hardwood sylva of his wide
range between the Great Lakes and the Gulf, the
prairies and the Atlantic. He has use for most of them.
In winter he digs up the caches of their nuts and seeds;
in spring he nibbles their shoots and buds; in summer
life to him is just a bowl of cherries, mulberries, hack-
berries, Juneberries, cornel berries, and fifty more. And
in autumn the whole forest is just one enormous nut,
for no other part of the world has so many wild nut
trees as this. When the pioneer children used to come
on nutting parties of their own, he would hang head
downwards on the trunk and scold them like a Dutch
uncle. His, *his* were every delicious black walnut,
every oil butternut, every starchy chestnut, every
luscious beechnut — *qua-qua-qua-qua-quack. Tcht!
Tcht! Tcht! Tcht! TCHT!*

But there is one kind of tree that the gray squirrel

has always loved above all other; wherever the hickories grow, there the gray squirrel from ancient time
has delighted to live, and where they are not found,
you find him rarely. Hickories are bound up no less
with the great traditions of our pioneering age. Of
hickory wood our ancestors made their wagon hubs
and felloes and shafts. Hickory bark was the first hinge
upon the cabin door, and roaring hickory logs fought
off the winter cold that besieged the cabin. Hickory
smoke cured our finest hams, and hickory ramrods sent
home the charge with which we stood off redskins and
redcoats. Straight as a mast, stronger than steel of the
same weight, shaggy of bark as a fringed hunting shirt,
it was the expression in wood of the rifle-cradling,
squirrel-hunting, Wilderness-trail American. He and
the gray squirrel loved hickory, that uniquely American tree, together; but when the virgin hickory was
mostly gone, an heroic human type went with it, and
the vast hordes of the gray squirrel (estimated at one
billion animals in the forest primeval) dwindled
swiftly, after 1870. And, as the squirrels vanished, the
hickories too failed to replace themselves as abundantly as before.

For almost every wild hickory, walnut, butternut,
pignut, and kingnut in this country was planted by a
squirrel. A tree, of course, in merely dropping its seeds
at its feet, cannot be said to *plant* them, to give them
that burial that means life renewed. Left on the sur-

face of the ground, their shells are so tough that in
many cases the germ of life inside would dry and
wither away before it could get enough moisture to
sprout. But the hoarding instinct of gray squirrels
leads them, as every child can bear witness, to bury
any nut they do not immediately consume; they not
only bury it but they pat the earth down around it
and strew the hiding place with leaves. This is all
done, no doubt, in unconscious selfishness, but if the
act were purposefully intended to renew the forest it
could not be better performed. True, the squirrel in-
tends to dig up again all the provender he has buried,
but who can doubt that he forgets or loses much of it
or dies at the hand of his natural enemies without ever
returning to claim his nuts?

And of all squirrels, the gray is the most efficient
tree planter, for he does not hoard his treasure all in
one chest but belongs to the one-nut-to-a-cache persuasion, and if he had studied at the Yale School of
Forestry he couldn't do better by the woods. Some
scientists believe that it was squirrels who speeded up
the reforestation of all the parts of North America
swept bare of life by the great ice sheets of the last
glacial age. That may be but a guess, yet I can think
of no likelier factor. If the trees had had to do it by
their unaided, tedious method of dropping their nuts
at their own feet, and waiting forty years or so for
their descendants to mature enough to do the same, it

is hard to see how they would have covered the vast glaciated territory in a million years; actually the elapsed time is estimated at a tenth of that.

The life of a gray squirrel usually begins at the end of winter, when mating is at its height, and continues in the mother's body for about forty-four days. Even after its birth, the gray baby knows little more of the world than he did in fetal life. He and his three or four brothers and sisters will not open their eyes for something like thirty-six days, and will be utterly dependent, weak, and helpless for eight or nine weeks, which is almost as long in proportion to a squirrel's span of days as is a human baby's helplessness in a man's. Gray babies are naked, their legs ridiculously short, their ears seemingly nonexistent, and the tail gives little promise of its future pride. Yet, as we say of a human brat, "His mother loves him," and gray squirrel mothers spend much time fondling their children. If a female has to abandon her den, she picks the babies up one at a time by the belly skin, while the youngsters wrap their tails around their mother's neck.

In all this this time they see nothing of their father. In the first place there is nothing he could do to be useful, since food is never brought to the den for the young; they are kept at the teat till abruptly weaned. In the second place, the male is by this time pursuing another mate. This is not resented by the first; she wouldn't tolerate him around the nursery anyway; his promiscuous behavior merely adds more little squirrels in the world, and who objects to that?

When a gray squirrel is big enough to walk and balance himself, his mother puts him away from her teats and he has to go and look for his own breakfast. He walks out on a limb and eats a few male catkins of the home nut tree. Then he tries tender buds and shoots. He is beginning to feel full of beans as a boy, pulls his sister's tail, is pursued by her, and dashes off with his well-known chuckle out on the farthest limb, takes his first jump across space, makes it (but barely) to the next tree, and sits up to look around. The fun has begun.

And Nature has fitted him superbly to enjoy it. He has big bright eyes, a nose that can smell anything good to eat from a grub to a hickory nut, and incisor teeth sharpened and flattened into chisels, while the low-crowned molars are like the undulations on the inside of a nutcracker. His forepaws are almost as mobile and cleverly manipulated for handling things as a raccoon's; his hind legs are coiled springs for jumping. His sharp nails let him cling to vertical trunks. And finally Nature has pinned on him that preposterous yet elegant tail. About his caudal appendage he is frankly vain. Other parts of him may get dirty or unkempt, but a patriotic fervor demands that he immediately remove from his national banner all sticks, mud, or gum. Some say he uses it for an extra blanket, and others as a parachute if he tumbles. He certainly talks with it as expressively as with his voice, erecting, jerking, rippling, and lashing it as the mood takes him.

Indeed, you seldom see a squirrel except in a state of high excitement, because he has almost always seen you first. For as soon as man enters his haunts there is a wild chattering on the squirrel telegraph line, and every brother, cousin, and aunt of the sentry either takes up the alarm, or scurries for cover. As you approach the little tattle-tale, he flattens himself out and sidles around the trunk. If you circle the tree, so does he, always keeping at least six inches of sound wood between you and him. If two hunters start in opposite directions around the tree, then he shoots straight up the trunk like an express elevator, taking refuge in his den.

But during several summers when I slept in a tent, I could observe and hear wild grays as they behave without consciousness of human beings around them. They did a surprising amount of talking, back and forth. There were soft contented barks, interspersed with humorous chuckles. Sometimes I heard a sound like smacking the lips over a feast, and again conversation in nasal grunts.

In his first winter, the gray squirrel really finds his voice in song. For that is the usual mating time. Part of the song reminds me of the sleepy notes of birds settling down in the dusk, or again it is like the thin peeping of a mouse. The sound may be hardly distinguishable from the creaking of boughs, yet sometimes the love song rises in seeming agony of longing to a machine-gun rattling, only to die away in rhythmical mewing.

Once in a squirrel lifetime, an impulse stronger than love's may overmaster him — a wild desire to leave home. There is no obvious reason why he should do so, for his den still promises to protect him from winter, no matter how severe, and the trees are heavy with his favorite foods. Yet he has to go, as surely as our pioneer ancestors had to pick up and move out west, when they felt the neighbors were settling in too close. But the emigrating squirrel doesn't go west exclusively; in some years he moves east, or south as readily. Whatever the call, he obeys it, traveling through the trees if he can, but bounding or waddling on the ground if need be. Never before has he voluntarily entered the water. Now not even the Mississippi, the Hudson, the Niagara, the Ohio stops him. He swims doggedly, emerging wet and miserable, but immediately takes up the road again.

Nor does he lack company, for every gray squirrel within a hundred miles is traveling with him, in the same direction. Studies in Ohio and Wisconsin have shown that these flights from nothing to nowhere occur in cycles of five years when the population has reached a peak of about 10.8 squirrels per acre. So we get a "squirrel year," and local gun clubs have high sport, by modern standards, when thousands of squirrels fill the woods. But in the old days not thousands but hundreds of thousands of squirrels descended like a plague of Egypt. A farmer might lose his entire corn crop in a single night.

"Simply incredible," "numbers past counting," "magnificent," "appalling," are the words used in the old accounts. Dr. Bachman, collaborator with Audubon on *The Quadrupeds of America* and a scientist whose word has never been doubted, went down the Ohio in 1809 when the river was strewn from bank to bank with gray squirrels crossing into Kentucky. He found the advancing front to be one hundred and thirty miles wide. A squirrel hegira in Ohio took fifteen days to pass a given point. Scientists have calculated some of these mad emigrations to have involved half a million gray pilgrims.

And mad they certainly were. They have been called migrations, but incorrectly, since a true migration involves a return trip to the breeding grounds. But the gray squirrels never return! So far as can be discovered, they travel on, till death overtakes them by hawk or fox, by drowning or lead. Neither the physiology nor the psychology of this suicide is understood. But it may be compared to the periodic march of the Norway lemmings which, when overpopulation crowds them in their mountain homes, travel downward to the sea and swim out into it until they perish.

Back in the homeland, from which the fated squirrels set out, the hunter, so studies have shown, will need an average of eleven and a half hours to bag one squirrel! But Nature will swiftly fill the void. Soon again in early spring every hollow tree will have its nursery of little suckling grays, preparing to start on their madcap existences, their nutty banquets. When summer comes, once more there will be a busy building of those airy treetop cottages of stick and leaf, where the happy-go-lucky squirrels will doze away the noontide heat. Again in fall these little foresters will go about their task of replanting the forest that gives them food and shelter. And once again the winter woods will rattle with this animated nutcracker's opinion of you: *Qua-qua-qua-qua-quack! Tcht, tcht, tcht, TCHT!*

TROUT COUNTRY

THERE WAS ONCE a dry-fly fisherman, so I've read somewhere, who was so eager to get a trout's-eye view of the angler's lures that he filled a bathtub, put his head under water and lay looking up while a friend cast on the surface an assortment of Silver Doctors, Zulus, Yellow Sallys, and Professors. When this anthropoid trout surfaced, he choked out news which it may pain you to hear. For he avowed he couldn't, when submerged, tell a Quaker from a Quack Doctor, or distinguish the bright hues of silk, tinsel, and feathers with which fishermen tie those lovely flies. All he could make out was a general black-and-white pattern, though he could perceive the motion of the lures more acutely than when he viewed them from above.

So that the exquisite artifacts of the fly-tier may not be wholly appreciated by the simple trout. Not that this matters much to the confirmed in the orthodoxy of dry fly. For the dry-fly purist is a serious-minded fellow whose stern moral fiber demands that he do things the hard way. He lets nothing distract him from his hobby. He will declare that the fool who takes his eyes from a strike because a flight of Canada geese goes honking grandly overhead, or lays down his rod to trace the odor of Mayflower to the pink corollas on the bank, is one you must remember to forget when the next fishing foursome is made up.

And yet I've noticed that of all sportsmen the anglers are the most observant of Nature. They can, for instance, spend hours analyzing their luck, and inevitably this involves a lot of entomology. They are generally good botanists too and can tell a spruce from a fir, and both from a pine. Far more than most city folks are they ornithologists, who never mistake a kingfisher for a bluejay. Well informed already, they seem always willing to learn more of the science of their art. So that perhaps they will let me, a mere naturalist, join the party in these pages. And chime up in the old arguments as to what makes a good trout stream, and whether golden trout are just a form of rainbows, and when and why fish rise — and all the rest. For I, too, love a trout stream, love the chill pure world that trout inhabit wherever you find them, love the fine country — forest or mountains — that alone can cradle these highborn waters.

Indeed, who could help loving trout country? For,

as he is a nobleman among fishes, so naturally the trout inhabits an aristocratic neighborhood — palatial, indeed — a world of quicksilver and rushing music, contrasting suddenly with the silence and stillness of those leaf-brown pools where alder and beech and birch lean over. Such streams, you will allow, are the sweetest waters that move on the face of our planet.

"Stream," of course, is too large a word for our purposes, unless we scale it down. The dictionary is disposed to include in the term anything from a rill to a current in the ocean. Yet rills are for minnows and children, the Grand Banks for commercial fishermen and mackerel. And your big, sluggish, muddy river is for the farmer's spiritless trotline. But a trout stream is white water, as the canoemen call it — living, singing, falling water, a young stream in the geologist's meaning of the word, never too far from its birthplace between the granite ribs of the hills, that has not worn itself down to a humdrum level.

These youthful qualities all trout streams have in common. Yet every angler knows that no two are identical, and even one may suffice for a lifetime of study, since it is never the same around two bends. The same pool at different hours of the day may have as many moods as the face of the woman you know best. No wonder the Greeks and Romans peopled their streams with female divinities — naiads and Nereids — to account for the fickle charms of running water. Woman-like, a trout stream, though of necessity it is small — a brook, a creek, a slim river — is the secret in the heart of the rodsman who knows it; its fame is private. Yet those best celebrated are known, half a world away, to men who have never seen them.

Thus, though history gives but a nod in the direction of the Test and the Itchen, they are held in reverence by all good disciples of the Great Ike, even though we may never cross the ocean to drop an angle in his famous chalk streams. Eastern fishermen who have read at all know of the Pacific-flowing Campbell and Kamloops, and their steelheads and cut-throats, and of the three K's of the Sierra Nevada, the Kings, the Kern, and the Kaweah, where dwell the golden trout. Westerners know of and envy the squaretails of the St. Anne and the Nipigon, the "brookies" — *fontinalis*, the speckled — of the Neversink and the Beaverkill. Those are names you won't find on a big map, but they make the fisherman hear the trip hammering of their falls, and see behind closed lids the sun-sprites on their riffles.

What — besides plenty of trout — makes a trout stream what it is? First of all, of course, it is cold water, never above 65°F., though the brown trout, an introduced foreign species, can take it somewhat warmer. Such a stream could scarcely run farther south than 40° north latitude. Or if farther south, then it is found only in high mountain waters.

And a trout stream is pure. It never normally carries

mud — only clean sand, gravel, and stones. It must not contain sewage, since that would soon exhaust the oxygen supply, replacing it with poisonous carbon dioxide. Trout demand great quantities of sweet oxygen forever passing over those blood-rich gills of theirs. To yield enough for their requirements, such a stream must "swallow" air, by leaping over falls and dancing down riffles. Not only the trout but his living fodder needs aerated waters. I recall in my student days trying to raise some of the larval and nymphal forms of trout insects in my aquarium. The water was cold and pure, yet my captives died before my eyes, of suffocation.

The ecologist — the fellow who studies the relations of organisms to their environment and to each other — divides up water life under two headings, the lotic and the lenitic. Lotic waters are those forever washing their beds and shores and all that in them dwells — either the surf zone of the oceans and great lakes, or the swift waters of streams. The lenitic are the still waters — of marshes, ponds, and the lakes and seas below the action of waves. Comparatively, the variety of plants and animals in lenitic waters is immense. The lotic societies, by contrast, are poor in species. In swift waters the company, as it were, is highly select, because it is selected from such few creatures as can live under the perpetual pressure of icy water and from the cleanly, sparse food cupboard of the trout stream. Many sorts of fishes could not even swim in white water, for the very shape of those with strongly flattened sides would preclude it; in a rushing current they would be caught broadside and spun around and around. To get ahead there you have got to be a stout fellow; trout, and the choice little company they keep, of fallfish and stonecats, chubs, darters, shiners, and brook minnows, are all rather broadly built, approaching the cylindrical in cross-section or even surpassing it, with bulging sides.

It is the same with lotic plants; the rank and spongy vegetation of the marsh, like cattail and duckweed, could keep no footing in tumbling water. Instead you find the wild mermaid tresses of the blue-green algae, the dark fontinalis moss streaming from the stones, and the riverweed which has had to give up all roots in favor of a holdfast, and looses its pollen on the flood.

To realize what the current pressure means in the life of lotic creatures, let's pull on our hip boots and wade into the stream. Say that it's the opening of the season, with the license, a bright if promissory note, still crackling in your breast pocket. The day has not yet made up its mind whether to go back to snowing or burst into trout lilies. Whether they bloom or not, their leaves are thrusting up sleek tongues through the loam on the bank, bearing those brown spots under the silver sheen that are as pat a resemblance and neat a bit of timing as you will find in Nature, not excepting shadblow and the run of shad.

Released from its prison of ice, the water lifts its voice in a seething brawl, like children bursting out of school. It is a sound that drowns all else. You can *see* the feathers trilling on the song sparrow's throat, his bill opening for that sputtering jingle; but all you hear is the lordly racket of the chutes.

You wade in. The footing is terrible; rocks where last summer you stood high-dry are trembling seismically now under ten inches of rollicking snow-melt. Even the bedrock is a polished treachery of slime from the winter crop of diatoms, those glassy microscopic plants that are the pasturage of so many stream dwellers. The vicious current tackles you around the legs, and you wonder if you will not be in it any minute, your creel afloat.

If this is how the current seems to us, imagine what it means in the lives of all that small fry that may weigh, individually, scarce more than a postage stamp, and yet must cling on with limpet desperation. Literally, the current streamlines what it washes. The forms of almost all lotic animals, from the leeches to the curious little lungless salamanders of swift water, are boat-shaped, fore and aft. Often they are flattened top-and-bottom fashion, as in the case of many of the bottom-crawlers, the larval stages of insects, with the legs coming out sideways, the rim of the body pressed close to the rock, the very heads flat as limpet shells.

In addition, every lotic creature must have extraordinary means of holding on tight, or fighting upstream. In the latter class, there is not a grander sight than the upstream run of the steelheads as they leap high from the thundering rapids and, describing a desperate parabola, plunge in, to appear again, gaining foot by fighting foot. But the creatures that cannot swim must cling tight. They find many ways of doing it. Some of the caddis worms weight themselves down with extra-heavy pebbles on the outside of the little cases they construct around their soft forms. The leeches cling on by means of sucking caps; some fishes hold their ground by stiff pectoral fins like braces. Many of the insect creepers have grasping jaws or grasping legs. That "black moss," as the angler is apt to call it, is really an undulating carpet of blackfly larvae whose bodies, at full stretch from their holdfast, stream out, plant-like, in the current. Certain caddisfly worms sometimes attach themselves, like spiders, by a silken life-line spun from their mouths. When they have to set out in search of food, carrying before them a little silken net for seining out the microscopic life swept on the current, they can always retreat on their guy-line if the going gets too tough.

Early spring at the trout stream is the wet-fly fisher's holiday, of course, since all the best trout food is in the submerged "creeper" stage. But suppose we come back to the stream a month later. No longer out of bounds, it flows sweetly as Afton. Now you can hear the chuckle of the wren above the gurgle of the whirl-pool. The water thrush is back; you hear his angelic voice bright in the clerestory of the young leafage, now upstream, now down it, always out of sight. Yet if you are still a moment, the singer, a brown bird with speckled breast and white line through the eye, will drop down confidingly on some near rock and, bob-bing and curtseying constantly, forage in the slack. The rattling kingfisher is back on his perch; but don't mind him too much; remember he can only catch the one that got away from you, and half the time is after crayfish. If you gaze fixedly down the creek you may see the solitary sandpiper, ambling delicately on the little sandy coasts, pretending, but only pretending, to ignore you. The wind brings the scent of sun-steeped resin. And the trout are rising after natural hatch.

The angler calls it this because caddisflies, black gnats, mayflies and craneflies seem to be materializing right out of the water, as if by spontaneous generation. Sometimes they may be dropping down from the sky for just one swift kiss of the stream. But in many in-stances the adults are actually getting "born" before our eyes. For it is another condition of life in swift waters that the creeper or worm, when it turns into a winged adult, frequently floats to the top and in the same instant splits its case and leaps right into flight. If it did not do so, the current would engulf it before it ever knew the joys of mating. If it is not swift enough, it meets a speedy death, announced by that familiar *blurb* that is a rising trout.

When this is happening all over the stream, it's more than the fisherman's flesh can bear. He takes a quick look in his fly-book, selects what most resembles the late lamented victim, and the battle of wits is on.

Wit — but who is joking which? Is the fish really deceived? Or is he too stupid to be fooled, and so merely strikes at anything? Or is he capable of becoming, if he has been hooked a few times, an "educated" trout, who can see through the whole trick and isn't having any?

The confirmed dry-fly worshiper is not too troubled for an answer. He has his faith in Royal Coachmen and Bivisibles, and faith is impressive even to skeptics. He has, too, his own picturesque nomenclature. When he talks of a drake (for mayfly) or a dun (for caddisfly) he is just as much within his Adamite rights to name the beasts as anyone. Naturalists and fishermen begin to misunderstand each other only when a "spinner" may mean a cranefly to one angler, a mayfly to another, and, to a third, some member of the zoologist's order of Megaloptera. Nor is the famous name of yellow sally tethered by agreement amongst all fisherman to one sort of insect. Small matter; the rodsman sometimes knows more than certain museum scientists that one sort of yellow sally flits across the pools on warm evenings, the purple drake on cool mornings, the cow-dung fly on breezy days, the sandy dun on cloudy ones.

Spring slips sweetly into early summer. Middays are apt to be oppressively hot and midgy. The rain crow, our American cuckoo, stutters his sultry notes; the drugging odor of wild basswood blossoms is on the breeze, and the trilling of toads is heard in the land. At the stream there are sharp changes — new species, and new habits. During the heat of the day many of the insects now hide under the suddenly too-heavy foliage. Yet when evening comes, they drop down, cranefly and mayfly, in their nuptial dances.

Mayflies, you don't have to remind the fly-tier, are known by the fact that they hold their pale little wings and the rear segments of their soft bodies, and their long tail bristles, erect when they are at rest. Thus you can tell them from the leggy craneflies which keep their big spotted wings and their short tails held hori-zontally. Well has the zoologist named the mayflies Ephemerids. Out of their annual life cycle they have but four or five days of adult life, during which they partake, with their weak mouth parts, of no food. They live only to mate, by the thousands. As twilight darkens the trout stream, you may see them descending in a swarm from the sky, till they tempt fate and trout by just touching the water before they bounce up in the air to disappear at thirty feet or so. For half an hour at most the dance goes on, only to vanish as suddenly as it materialized.

The craneflies are only less numerous than mayflies, and a lot more conspicuous by size. The fisherman has named for them his Whirling Spinner and Golden Spinner and many another lure with a pretty name. Most of the individuals you will see in the courtship dance are males, for they divert themselves in swirling eddies before the females have emerged from their pupal cases on the shore. There the males wait for them, seizing them as soon as they are "born," and off they fly together, the female dragging her mate behind her in a tandem honeymoon. Sometimes they stoop low to the water; sometimes they hover, never unclasping, to sip a dainty wedding feast at the nectars of flowers. When egg-laying time comes on, the female hovers over the water, stabbing it like the needle of a sewing machine with her ovipositor. That's the trout's last chance at spinners, for one summer at least.

Summer? Well, the full tide of it finds many of our trout streams closed to fishermen by the game laws. Time to pack up your tackle then and travel north, or try the High Sierra's tiny scattered lakes that glitter as cold and bright as the winter constellations. But wherever you go, trout country is good country. Maybe a farmer wouldn't say so, or city money-makers. It's no good for raising corn, no good for suburban developments, no good for oil wells, and a hundred other oh-so-worthy things. In fact it's sweetly good for nothing — except the best things on earth: a white stream and a tall spruce, a tight line, a game fight, a flash of living silver — and a grill above a fragrant fire. Things worth remembering, these are, in the long count of the short days.

JACK RABBIT

COUNTRY

JACK RABBIT COUNTRY means a lot of country — and a lot of rabbits. It might be found almost anywhere from western Wisconsin to the badlands of Washington, from central Texas to southern California. And a long way south in Mexico. For Jack, the king of hares, surveys a vast domain and calls it his. Extremes of temperature, heavy snowfall, rainfall and lack of rainfall, all seem to make slight difference to him. He prefers a plain, or a rolling mesa, but is found up to twelve thousand feet in some of our desert ranges, and below sea level in Death Valley. His food plants are — almost anything which grows. He prefers his footing

dry, and sidesteps the dews and damps of long grass and bosky woods. Yet there is one thing all good jack rabbit regions have in common, and that is opportunity for the play of his two chief weapons for survival — speed and concealment. So Jack's land is brushland — open brush with short grass between.

True, "Brer Rabbit," so Uncle Remus tells us, was "bawn and bred in de briah patch." But, then, Brer Rabbit was a cottontail, a *Sylvilagus* (wood rabbit); he was not a *Lepus* — our jumping jack, the roughneck of rabbits, the original, I should think, of "Bugs Bunny." In the briary bush, those preposterous long ears would catch and tear; those mighty hind legs, like coiled springs, could not deploy their power of bounding motion. For him, then, no dense forest undergrowth, no intricate, twiggy chaparral. Equally, he eschews barren sands and mountain rocks without cover to hide him from his foes, the hawk and wolf. But sagebrush, in the northwest, exactly suits the white-tailed jack. In the southwest, cactus desert favors the antelope jack, while mesquite and creosote-bush are the natural home of the black-tailed jack.

The last is the bunny I know best. I know and love the country where he lives. Men call it desert, but it is not deserted. I never saw so many animals per mile, or per hour, in my life as by the light of my car, driving slowly through the desert night over the washboard ranch roads. It is a poor sixty seconds when no lizard

or gopher or pack rat or jumping mouse scurries
through the beam of your headlights. Or a jack rabbit
— most of all, jack rabbits. Even in the blaze of a
desert noon when the jacks are resting in the shade of
the creosote-bushes, you can rouse one from his siesta
every few minutes by walking boldly through the
brush. And animal life of other sorts abounds by day.
There is a hummingbird or a butterfly for every flower.
Flowers on the desert, you ask? Yes, in spring, after a
late snowfall, millions of them, fields of them, miles of
them, rolling away to the horizon like a delicately
colored carpet to the rim of the world and over the
rim.

I once made a collection of specimens gathered
within fifteen minutes' walk of Yucca Loma Ranch on
the Mohave. A catalogue of this herbarium tells me
that I found just one hundred and one species — almost as many as an equally small tract in flowery New
England or lush Illinois prairie would yield. These
little swift-sprung annuals bore such names as dande-
lion, buckwheat, daisy, marigold, four-o'-clock, forget-
me-not, blazing-star and rock pink — though it is not
to be understood that they represented the same
flowers we call by those names in other places. With
lupine and larkspur, gilia and sand verbena, they filled
every inch of space — for the brief weeks of their
blooming — between the creosote-, paperbag, burro,
and rabbit bushes.

Cactus there was, of several kinds, and highly important to jack rabbits, as I shall show, but nothing compared to the variety and sheer numbers one sees in Arizona; the Mohave is definitely not a cactus desert. If one kind of growth should be selected to typify it, that would be the creosote-bush, named for the odor of the tiny evergreen leaves, which smell very strong when the sun comes out after a shower. Its immense success in jack rabbit country can be attributed to two factors — it is about the only vegetation on the desert that jack rabbits don't devour, and it can go for as much as two years without a drop of moisture. But if Jack does not relish this bitter bush, he appreciates the shade and concealment of its twiggy sprawling domes of growth, and finds it seldom more than a few joyful or fearful leaps from one creosote-bush to the next.

Now, if this picture of the western Mohave does not coincide with your previous notions of desert, remember that there are as many kinds of desert as there are types of forest. Maine woods and Ozark woods, Florida woods and California woods are all forest — but alike in nothing. So why must all deserts be Saharas, with dunes, camels, date palms, and Bedouins? In this country we have many sorts — the Painted desert, the Great Salt Lake desert, the Gila desert, to mention but a few. The western Mohave, where the black-tailed jack abounds, even has a river, and a forest! Naturally, neither is like forest and river elsewhere. The stream, called "the river of Buenaventura" in old Spanish tales, was supposed to flow from California to the Mississippi. The explorer, Captain John C. Frémont, led by the immortal Kit Carson, exploded that myth a century and more ago. But a river there is, the Mohave, fed only by the mountains' melting snowcaps (something like the "canals" of Mars); in glacial times it forced its way two hundred miles, to Death Valley and there formed a lake. Today, braiding its way in silver strands, lined with cottonwoods that mock you with the sound of pattering rain, it disappears in mid-Mohave in an alkali playa.

As for the forest, it is made up of one kind of tree — a tree without solid wood or true bark, a tree without shade, a tree whose age cannot be determined, though it must be great, since I have never heard of anyone who saw a Joshuatree grow an inch. Yet it is a tree in height and form — a grotesquely branching yucca with huge, globular, waxy flowers. Like all other growth in jack rabbit country, Joshuatrees stand far apart. You can see right through a Joshua grove — which does not deny it the right to be called a forest, for wherever you look, in, say, the Joshuatree National Monument, these unearthly trees encompass you like a bristling host.

That's jack rabbit country for you, and though it is desert, I know of no other field laboratory so ample, so uncluttered, yet so full of life you can easily see and study. The botanizing is the most interesting, the "bird-ing" the easiest, I have ever encountered. And hunting there should certainly be, for the sportsman, the most unrestricted. After all, there is no bag limit on jack rabbits, the bane of the alfalfa farmer and the rancher who hoards every blade on the range. And there is no closed season; why should there be? There are always black-tailed jacks and there always will be.

Perhaps we should stop and get Jack straight with our zoology. Strictly speaking, he is not a rabbit but a hare. The true rabbits are born blind and naked. The black-tailed jack comes into this world dressed to step right out in it without embarrassment, in a full suit of fur. And, sensible child, he is born with eyes wide open. They had better be, in a country swarming with slinking coyotes and swift prairie falcons and lurking rattlers. However, he is a "rabbit" in common par-lance and in a wide sense, and he received the name of jackass rabbit, for those donkey ears, when in the Mexican War our troops first encountered him as they marched to California. Shortened to jack rabbit, the name has stuck, and would wound the feelings of a purist only.

The jack rabbit is a wonderful animal. There are people who can see wonder only in that which is rare or fantastic. But surely this creature, who has every man's hand against him, who is levied on unmercifully to satisfy the ravenous hunger of coyotes, gray wolves, desert foxes, skunks, weasels, kingsnakes, rattlesnakes, badgers, golden eagles, prairie falcons, red-tailed hawks, must have what it takes to survive, and not only survive but abound. If he is common animal, he possesses uncommon and uncanny equipment to endure where his flesh and blood are the chief answer to the cruel hunger and thirst of the desert.

First there is his jumping power. A blacktail jack was seen by one zoologist to jump a five-and-a-half-foot "rabbit-proof" fence — not driven to extraordinary exertions by fear, but merely in order to get at the farmer's crops on the other side. The white-tailed jack, they say, will cover twenty-two feet and four inches at a leap. That's going places! A black-tailed jack will bound on and on for miles, on those tireless springs of his, fifteen feet at a bound, two hundred hops a minute, says one naturalist; I once clocked Jack at thirty-five miles an hour, by the speedometer of my car, as he loped parallel to the highway. The coyotes do not live who can run that fast. They have to place reliance on their sneaky tread, as they steal up on sleeping jacks or helpless jack youngsters.

In jumping, Jack usually rises about two feet off the ground, smacking the earth with all four feet at once and close together. In full flight for his life, though, he leaps much higher, for he knows what every artilleryman knows — that to hit more distant targets you have to raise the trajectory of the shell. Some of the highest jumps are probably "spy hops" — the creature looks over his shoulder, as he clears the brush, to take note of the nearness and the direction of the pursuit. If a pack of pursuers tries to run him into the jaws of others, these reconnaissance flights betray the enemy strategy, and he can change direction in a flash.

And those mulish ears! How we laugh at them — bigger in proportion to Jack's head than a donkey's to its own poll. They give the bunny the most asinine expression, and so we think him a zany. But he needs every inch of them. Twisting them sensitively this way and that, he uses those ears like so many antennae for collecting out of the air sounds which you and I catch not at all. There is a Russian proverb that says "Fear has big eyes," but in rabbitdom it wears big ears.

Jack is protectively colored, too. In various parts of his vast range, he takes on different hues; out on the Mohave, where washed-out browns and faded grays are the commonest shades in the landscape, he dresses to merge with the brown of the earth, the gray of the creosote-bushes' stems. When cowering in concealment, he lowers his ears till they cover his head and are streamlined with his body. If you look right at him as he moves about, he "freezes." You may wonder why he imagines you can't see him; but probably you frequently do look right at jack rabbits without seeing them. If you move quietly toward him he takes a short flight, then turns sidewise and watches you with one eye. Many a hunter has imagined that his next bound will be straight ahead, but in all likelihood it will not; if startled a second time, he spins round in a high bound and dashes through the brush. It's a quick Nimrod who gets a shot at him then.

Much of Jack's life is lived at night — another weapon of defense. Then it is he commits his most unhindered depredations on the rancher's alfalfa. Then it is he gets his courting done; few people, in consequence, have ever seen wild jack rabbits mating. I admit I have not done so, though I once saw two males fighting. They stood up and boxed, and the sound of the vicious blows came distinctly, something like the sound of spanking a dog. The worst blows, however, were ripping strokes, dealt with a hind leg, and tearing out fur. The front paws were used for sparring. If I hadn't come so close as to break up the fight, one of them would probably have disemboweled the other.

Spring is the height of the mating season, but young have been found in pregnant females every month in the year. In the warm parts of the country there may be three or four litters a year, and one to five bunnies at a litter; the average is three. Nothing sensational, that, compared with guinea pigs, but enough — and plenty, thinks the farmer. If every female had three young to a litter and three litters year then, in ten years, nine hundred jack rabbits would flourish where one had been before.

And still we haven't come to Jack's most wonderful equipment. The problem of every desert dweller is water. Mesquite roots travel hundreds of feet in following the least vein of it. Doves, clipping off a mile-a-minute flight, fly sixty or a hundred miles to drink, twice a day. In the early days of exploration, our army engineers carefully mapped every water hole, and even today you have to think about water before you set out in your car. A boiling engine, a leak in the radiator, may be serious, in mid-Mohave and midsummer. With all those millions of jack rabbits on the desert, where do they find enough to drink — especially as they seldom voluntarily travel more than a couple of miles from their birthplace?

The answer is that Jack simply doesn't have to drink. He may live a whole rabbit-span of existence without tasting free water!

This is true of many other desert animals. The burrowing owls, who nest underground, get all the water they need from the tiny pocket mice. The pocket mice, however, do not drink either; they get their water from eating seeds. The seeds, too, never get wet, until the moment they are ready to sprout; they are almost as dry as the wood of the desert shrubs, which are eaten by the powder-post beetles — who in their turn never drink.

But there is some water, however undetectable the quantity, in every bit of living tissue. What little there is in the jack rabbit's food is hoarded, for this hare probably perspires little or not at all. More, these teetotaling desert dwellers actually produce water in their own systems. This is called the water of metabolism.

To understand it, we have to remember that metabolism, in man or a jack rabbit or a burrowing owl, is a burning or consuming by means of oxygen. And it is one of the oddities of all forms of burning that you cannot have fire without giving rise to water. For the chemical sum of adding oxygen to any carbohydrate is to burn up the carbon, and release the hydrogen. Combined with the oxygen, it makes water. In the open air this water would pass off unperceived as water vapor. But in the body of a desert animal it is captive, like the water in a sealed radiator. It can be circulated round and round in the system. It is the answer to the first and eternal problem of the desert.

Jack rabbits, in their choice of food, have one resource of abundant water that seems incredible to human beings, when we consider the delicacy of those twitching noses of theirs: they eat cacti! Many animals employ cacti in various ways. The cactus wren delights to build her barrel-shaped grass nest deep in the most horrendous array of the terrible jumping cholla's spines. There is no human hand could pluck forth her precious eggs, and I have never seen any sort of bird or quadruped attempt to invade this stronghold. The trade rats — those elvish rodents who steal anything you have and always leave you something you don't want in exchange — are said to line the openings of their big untidy nests (that look like flotsam on the beach) with a curtain of land mines in the form of balls of cholla spines. But the jack rabbit beats all, by delicately worming his snout in among the stiff thorns of the barrel cactus; once he can get his chisel teeth into the epidermis of this vegetable water-barrel he has triumphed. He begins to eat from the top of the columnar cactus downward; he simply guts the inside, leaving the cuticle of the rifled plant helpless, for all its armament, on the desert floor.

With nibbling capacities like this, it is no wonder that Jack is indicted by ranchers and farmers with a long list of charges. Some estimates have put the damage of these hares to the range grasses as one third the total pasturage and browse. An acre of alfalfa — the desert's best crop — may be cut down in a few nights, during years of rabbit abundance. Traps, poisons, rabbit-proof fences have all been employed; sometimes they do some good. But the most effective and most brutal method of control is by organized drives. A great circle of farmers and their families beat the bush and drive the terrified hares into a stockade. The gate is closed and then — well, you've seen the rest in newsreels; men and even children, armed with clubs, enter the stockade and beat the poor wretches to death. As a form of pest extermination it may be justified; as a sight it is about as unedifying as any kind of massacre of the helpless. And above all, I hate to hear it called sport.

Your real sportsman hunts his jack rabbits where they have a chance. Probably no shooting except quail shooting, when the quail "bomb" explodes, requires such quick reactions, such split-second marksmanship, as when old Jack-the-blacktail unexpectedly bounds out of a bush, and whirls away with antelope speed. And no other form of shooting of any kind of true game animal can be done with such a free conscience. The sport is great, the flesh is fair eating, the farmer benefits, and there are always more blacktails. As for the victim, a clean shot through the head is a happier fate than the others that await him — to be torn to pieces by coyotes, or borne off in the cruel claws of a redtail, or flogged to death in a corral.

Justice, science, and common sense demand that we give Jack his due. Beside being a pest he is also a distinct asset — quite aside, that is, from the value of his pelt which sells for about seven cents a hide to the makers of felt hats and inexpensive fur coats. For Jack's place in the economy of Nature is a vital one. He acts as a "buffer species," as the biologists say. That is, he bears the greatest share of the food needs of all the creatures that prey on him. When the rabbit population falls too low — due to epidemics of disease or an increase in coyotes — then finer creatures than he must suffer. One of the finest of these is that little beauty of a game bird, the desert or Gambel's quail, who immediately begins to be victimized by the hawks. Coyotes, too, turn more attention to calves and deer. Then the stockmen call for a coyote extermination campaign, the coyotes dwindle, and Jack jumps up again.

Jack rabbit country is fine country, that frees the spirit with its great, clear spaces. You will love it for the depths of its silence — as great by day as in the night. Even the wind blows there without finding much to whistle about; it comes sweeping out of the skies as a big push, and nothing more. You will love it for the cool dream of snowcaps on its ranges, and for the way you can see there; ranges fifty miles away open long gaps, like the scenery in a Dali painting, to show others fifty miles farther, and just as sharp and shining, as if cut out of metal. You will love it for the bare white dawns, full of the dry *chuff-chuff-chuff* of the cactus wrens, for its astronomical sunsets when the red ball drops from a cloudless sky behind the mountains and their long shadows, like the penumbra of some eclipse, go rushing eastward to join and make the night. You will love the nights for their stars, for the long quavering songs of coyote choral societies, and the sweet tooting of a burrowing owl, sitting contentedly at his door. You will like the twilight best, though, when the nighthawks sweep the skies with a

soft purring sound, and the great white desert prim-
roses and the gilias called evening-snow open their
corollas and release their delicate fragrance.

Twilight is the blacktail's favorite hour too, for
though seen at any hour, he is always seen in greatest
numbers at dusk. The hawks have left the sky, the
coyotes and rattlers are not yet in full prowl. This is
Jack's hour for feeding at peace and, one would say,
for play and relaxation after his siesta. There goes one!
and another seems to leap up from the same spot, and
dash in another direction. Probably it's a mated pair
(well, mated for the moment; we won't go into the
blacktails' morals), with young nearby. For it is the
way of these parents to crouch near, but not too near
their youngsters. Then, if something approaches, they
draw attention by rushing off distractingly. If you
hunted about, you would probably find the cowering
bunnies, who look quite unlike their parents, with small
ears and snubby faces. But why scare the poor kids?
They have a lifetime of terror ahead of them, alter-
nating with the boldest deviltry. But they live it full
tilt, and the vanishing scut which is the last you see of
Jack is really the flag of a triumphantly successful
species.

VALLEY QUAIL

COUNTRY

Just to say the two words, valley quail, is to pronounce the name of the best-dressed upland game bird native to America. It is to raise up in the memory of anyone who ever saw him the jaunty, dandified figure of a sporting bird, who has against him every predator that runs or flies or wriggles on the ground, and yet, with

sportsmanly instinct, by guile and wile, by speed and mother-wit, gives every sort of hunter, from human to hawk, a baffling chase.

I first saw this famous bird in his still more famous habitat when I had been in California only a few hours and was viewing a house I was minded to rent. The situation was superb, halfway up a mountain whose tops were crowned with redwood forests, while at its feet the blue arms of San Francisco Bay wound among the hills turned brass and bronze in the summer drought. And even as I took my first deep look, the corner of my eye detected motion; I turned my full gaze and beheld a startling apparition that had just stepped out of the bushes in a self-conscious manner, as if it were deliberately drawing my attention from something else, something importantly secret. About the size of eastern bobwhite (say, ten inches long), he was a rich gray-blue on back and wings, the flanks flecked with white dashes like ermine tails, the underparts patterned in black-bordered scales and washed with cinnamon. On his throat he wore a broad bib of velvety black edged with a U-shaped band of white. A milk-white line passed above his eyes like a headband and went down the sides toward the nape where rode a restless, scaly, pepper-and-salt mantle.

This fancy-dress appearance was capped by a topknot of broad-ended feathers that bobbed forward between his eyes at each mincing step, as he strolled with all the nonchalance of a tame bird accustomed to being admired. I actually looked around for bird-cages from which this dandy might well, I thought, have strayed. And in the seconds that my eyes were averted, he did a disapparing act as swift and complete as a rail's. I stepped toward the bushes where he must have vanished — and raised a bedlam of warning cries. They sounded like *Ah-rrrroo! Rooo-coook! Roo-COOO-cook!* Then a general alarm, knocked out on every side, of *Get-RIGHT-out! Get-RIGHT-out!*

There followed a terrific fussing, clucking, and pit-a-patting, and as I plunged into the shrubbery I flushed a whole flock, handsome males like the one I had seen and their more soberly costumed womenfolk. By twos and threes they rose and skimmed low with a soft whirr, and each time that I supposed them all flown, more kept rising from under my feet. I imagined that if I had had a dog to course them I could have run down the whole covey. Little did I know then of the bafflements and stratagems of that great sportsman, the valley quail.

Now I have grown accustomed to waking to the morning clarion of this gamy neighbor: *Get-RIGHT-up! Get-RIGHT-up!* Sometimes he crows it sweetly from the vacant lots around my house, sometimes startlingly loud in the very vines that clamber around my bedroom window. I know his nests, and the beautiful mottled and scrawled-over eggs; I know his chicks, like toddling black balls of fluff. I know his country which may be anywhere in the Golden State except the deserts, high mountains, and tall timber. For valley quail is the prime game bird of what the tourist calls, whether in derision or admiration, "sunny California." That means the part with the Mediterranean type of climate; it means old Spanish California, the California of the missions strung like pearls on the *camino real*, the royal highway, approximated today by U.S. Highway 101. It is the California of ancient live oaks and fields sheeted, in spring, with blue of lupine and orange of poppies, of white-cliffed headlands jutting into the sapphire of the Pacific.

If I could choose one spot more than any other that should be of the very type and instance of valley quail country, it would be a bit of deserted coast that I get away to every spring. To reach it I have to drive twenty miles up the coast highway, turn off it on a smaller road for ten miles, turn off again on a winding narrow byway for another ten, take a bumpy ranch road for a mile, and come to a stop atop a long slope, in sight of the ocean. Curved like a curlew's bill, the shore there stretches away and away to a spick-and-span lighthouse in the east, a final gleaming headland in the west. All the scene, indeed, looks as though the artist's paint were still wet on the canvas, so bright the faultless arch of sky and rolling Pacific, so primary the colors of the wild flowers — yellow and blue lupine and green of the range grass. It is a spot marvelously empty, even lonely; I never meet a soul there, and the occasional herds of white-faced Herefords look at me in surprise. Four times a day one of the California-poppy-colored streamliners comes wagging around the curves, whistling a deep Diesel warning and looking almost

like a toy train down there, forges its way over the un-
rolled rug of flower-streaked fields to vanish, leaving the
scene more lonely for its momentary presence. The
breeze, sweetly chill, runs through the grass, laying
about it with the flat of its sword. The sun, sweetly
warm, bakes from the brushland the minty tang of
sage, the wormwood smell of sagebrush. And then, on
the silence, from the depths of the brush, rings the love
song of the valley quail, a single note, half pleading,
half reproachful, *Coy!*

Not much of a song, you say? Nothing, certainly, to
compare with some others you can hear in valley quail
country — the sudden, glittering, jingling bursts of
meadowlarks sitting on the fence posts, or the reflec-
tive lay of the thrasher in the chaparral thickets, like
a mockingbird's but not so bold and showy, not de-
livered to an applauding audience, rather a hymn sung
in solitude, with only heaven and earth to hear. Yet in
that reiterant *coy* all that is left of the wild, in coastal
California, is concentrated. It is as if the voiceless part
of Nature — the sun-steeped brush, the deep *barranca*
where a stream made headway to the sea, the very earth
that bore the flowers — found itself in a solitary tone, as
a bell's single note expresses many things, a summons,
a beseeching, an hour of day, and yet the timelessness
of time forever passing.

Strangely, though, quail are actually easier to see,
and see in numbers, in the suburbs than out in the wild

where they have learned an ancient wariness, put on them by bobcats, gray fox, blue darters (Cooper's hawks), gopher snakes, skunks, weasels, and jays. Within the neighborhood of houses these constant and ravenous predators are less common. And, of course, no shooting is permitted within corporate limits. Indeed, quail there have the status of pets, and seem to know it. Though cautious always, a bevy of suburban quail will show itself many times a day, to affectionate human admirers. Some of these put out grain for them. When the chicks are hatched, motorists (who cheerfully run over quadrupeds of all sorts) take an unexpected care with quail, throwing on the brakes when they see them crossing the road, just as they would for school children.

From its tameness and seeming abundance around the haunts of man, you might imagine that *Lophortyx californica* was on the increase. In a certain sense it is, for sportsmen and game commissions have transplanted it in Oregon and Washington, Nevada and Utah. In regions of heavy snowfall to which it is ill-adapted, thousands of farmers scatter grain for it in winter, convinced not only of its charms but its value. But, offsetting completely any gains in area, are continuing losses both in territory and numbers. We do not have exact statistics on its former abundance, but all old-timers can remember when a single flock might number two thousand birds; today a flock of two hundred is considered large.

In the years 1895 and 1896, as many as 70,370 quail lay as corpses in the meat markets. Still earlier, 100,000 of these birds were annually shipped to San Francisco. Two hunters, in the fall of 1883, secured three hundred *dozen* in a seventeen-day hunt. One hunter took a hundred and fourteen birds in a single day. Hunters were paid a dollar a dozen and restaurants charged thirty cents for quail on toast. Two hunters are reported who built a brush blind near a spring in the Temblor Mountains where the birds were obliged, for miles around in those arid hills, to come for water. The ground all about was daily covered with a compact body of quails, and all the hunters had to do was to mow them down by the score at every discharge.

As the curve of quail population has declined to perhaps ten per cent of its former maximum, or perhaps dropped much more, the curve of human population has risen in California at an ever-steepening climb. This means a corresponding increase in the number of hunters, each of whom would like to have a go at the state's finest game bird. The result is that the legal bag and the season are constantly shortening. And that the quail are being crowded out of the only kind of country they can enjoy. For a vast acreage that once was ideal for them is now turned into grain fields or covered by those foreign weeds, black mustard and wild oats, or is overgrazed or burned off. The plow, the hunters assert, is deadlier to quail than the severest discipline of gunfire.

More and more streams are being diverted near the source for irrigation purposes. Once the landscape of coastal California was laced with countless creeks which ran the year around or nearly so. Today those beds are all too often white and dry as bones. Quail do not require much water, but they cannot live forever without it. They do not require much of Nature's wild harvest of seeds and grass, but they cannot, when those are taken away, adapt themselves to other foods, any more than you could live on what the quail eat. They cannot nest where no safe sites are left to them. They cannot crowd in with other flocks, for every acre of good quail country is already as full of quail as Nature allows. An evicted quail is a dead quail.

But nothing is so lively as a live one. Let us follow him into the brush. Daybreak finds the flock well up in the tops of young or medium-sized live oaks, whose bushy growth and evergreen leaves give the concealment that these birds must have, in a world of long-tailed hawks. The quail's day begins late (for a bird), since he hates the dew and waits for the first rays of the summer sun to lick the grass and bushes dry. Then he sends forth his crow that means, "Arise and shine!" Of a fine morning, out in the country, you can hear one

covey beyond another, passing this cheery word over
hill and hollow. The sound seems to travel to the edge
of morning, and then comes bouncing back to be tossed
on in turn. There is something that lifts the heart in
that glad racket; you discover that the air is fresh as
spring water and smells of eucalyptus and wood smoke;
you find that you feel wondrous healthy; you could
climb any height, tramp any length.

Their matins said, the flock begins to drop down out
of their roost; then they trot in some hurry to the
morning bath. This is a dusty hollow concealed by
young trees and tall plants. However safe it seems,
some of the old males mount sentry duty, to be re-
lieved one by one by other birds, until all have had a
thorough dust-shower, followed by a good shake-out
of the feathers.

It is now breakfast time, and if the season is summer
or autumn, the meal consists in only three per cent of
meat — spiders, snails, centipedes, and insects; all the
rest is seeds of such plants as the brilliant-flowering
chaparral pea, the wild morning-glory, sumac, crane's-
bill (geranium), sage, old-man or sagebrush, lupine,
coffeeberry, and even poison oak. Farm pests like
knotweed, filaree, bur thistle, tarweed, hoarhound, and
black mustard are freely eaten by this living weed-kil-
ler, as he pecks his way downhill, either silent or con-
versing in a guardedly low patter.

Always valley quail keep close to their favorite

brushland. This should not be mistaken for the intricately twiggy, head-high chaparral that covers such a large part of coastal California. Quail are not safe there, where they cannot maneuver by running or readily escape from the ground in flying. Nor are they found on wide expanses of pasture far from any concealment from that thunderbolt from the skies, the blue darter. No, their chosen ground is the old-man and the sage. This growth is not only rich in seeds, but it is just thick enough to give a flock concealment, just open enough to allow them to see, to maneuver, to forage, and to escape. Find sage, and you've found where quail are, or should be, if not driven out by thirst or hunger or overshooting.

Noon or earlier finds the little foragers at the bottom of the slope — almost always an eastward slope. If there is a bit of bottom-land there, or a deep *barranca* grown up to arrowweed, willow, and blackberry, they rest there, enjoying, like any other good aboriginal Californian, a short siesta or, if awake, loafing around like fellows with nothing much to do. Once the meridian is past, the flock will commonly begin to climb slowly up the opposite hill, the westward-facing side, enjoying the shadow in the heat of the day. Before sundown they will have reached the crest, and now, for the only time in the whole day unless flushed by an enemy, they fly — back to their nightly roost. This, by preference, is a live oak, though not usually

one of the grand, picturesque, two-hundred-year-old
specimens, but a young, vigorous, densely bushy one,
for such offer the best concealment. Here they settle
down, after a few calls and twitterings, for a long sleep.
If no tree rat or prowling cat comes stealing along the
boughs, that sleep is deep and uneventful.

When the winter rains come to California, about
Christmas time, all the landscape turns green, for winter in the Mediterranean-type climate is biologically
springtime. The air, between the rains which often
fall in the night, is chill but sparkling; again the clatter
of the creeks is heard; the earth has a delicious smell
of toadstools; the grass comes rushing up through the
soil, and swiftly a carpet of clover and filaree spreads
everywhere.

This is the season when the quail change from a diet
of seeds (since there are few left) to the tender shoots
of herbage. While feeding on it, though, they never
venture more than a few feet from brush or trees, so
fearful must they be of hawk, skunk, weasel, bobcats,
house cats, and gopher snakes.

In February or March the flocks break up in pairs
for mating. The males are monogamous, but all the
same fierce fighting over some favorite female has been
recorded. Once affairs are settled, the female makes
her nest. Normally it is placed on the ground and, like
other ground birds', it is a poor affair at best. (Some
hen quail will even impose on other birds like the gen-

tle towhee or the raucous roadrunner, and make them hatch the quail young.) As the female sits on her big clutch of white eggs scrawled and mottled with undecipherable characters, her mate mounts guard, twanging out his *coy*, or, in case of the approach of an enemy, he bravely shows himself and leads the chase away from his precious secret.

The precocial chicks step out of the eggs handsomely clothed in black down and all ready to run and scratch from the start. Ants forms a large part of their baby-food. When they can toddle tirelessly, parents and children begin once more to form into flocks with their neighbors. Since the birds are not polygamous, there is no cock-of-the-roost in a valley quail flock, and no leadership. On democratic lines families unite for mutual protection and society.

An idyllic life, by the sound of it. But of all the birds in California, the quail is the most relentlessly preyed upon. How little fun it would be to lead a valley quail's existence I accidentally demonstrated yesterday. I had started out with my quail-caller for a stroll through some vacant lots where I knew quail roosted at night. My whistle was but a feeble imitation of the heart-lifting wild call, but in five minutes I had collected two bird dogs, four lynx-eyed house cats, six squawking jays, and a pair of Cooper's hawks who kept stealing silently from tree to tree following the sound as I walked along. If with a rubber band and two little splints of wood I could convoke all these stealthy hunters, how harried must be the bird who cannot show topknot or speak to his mate without incurring the possibility of instant death! Chicks above all are in danger. The close students of the quail assert that of a dozen hatched in one month there will not, on the average, be half that number to arrive at adulthood. The mortality in eggs is quite as severe. And adulthood is but little protection. Most quail are destined to die violent deaths, against which they have no weapons of defense.

But guile they certainly possess. I have seen it again and again, and every hunter has a reluctantly admiring tale to tell of the way the valley quail fooled him. I have heard it said by eastern bobwhite hunters that they do not like our quail because, after being flushed, they will not "lie to the dog," that is, freeze still on the ground until Rover can raise them for another shot by his master. And indeed if what you want is a bird that is little trouble to bag, then the valley quail is not for you.

For our California *Lophortyx* when flushed does not explode like a bomb, as bobwhite do, but comes whirring and boiling up in pairs and in threes. If the hunter succumbs to the temptation to set off after the first few, he leaves many birds behind, and these will then fly in the opposite direction. If they take refuge in an oak they immediately run along the branches to the opposite side. When the hunter approaches the tree, he hears the whir of their departing wings, but he has a dense screen of leafage between him and the shot. They may fly half a mile, taking care if they can to put the crest of a hill between the gun and the spot where they alight. But even if you can mark it, you will seldom find the quarry there. Since they have not risen again, where, you wonder could they have gone?

If I hadn't seen a bevy come flying toward me, for their lives, their topknots low down on the heads, I could hardly believe the accounts I have read. As they lit, they broke into a run almost as fast as their flight, which is estimated sometimes as high as twenty-five miles an hour. It was like watching an airplane land and then go rushing down the strip on its wheels. Hunters say the birds will run another half mile before they stop.

If thoroughly frightened, valley quail may eventually freeze, but when they do they can disappear in three wisps of vegetation, and by the time they do so, say the hunters, the dog is exhausted and no use at all. Truly, the human who matches wits with valley quail and wins, will, when he goes to heaven, be found in the constellation of Orion.

It is no wonder that valley quail was chosen by a radio poll to be the state bird of California. True, the sportsmen didn't care much for the idea; they were afraid (groundlessly, as it seems) that if *Lophortyx* became the bird emblem, sentiment might force it off the list of legal game. Many school children preferred the merry meadowlark; the ornithologists were plugging the bubbling wren-tit because he is found throughout the state. But an unclassifiable tide of voters slowly welled up who carried the day for the bird with the jaunty topknot. California once chose the grizzly bear as its emblem and then made him extinct. May it better revere the valley quail and let him, in his own words, "Stay-RIGHT-here!"

WOODCHUCK

COUNTRY

IF YOU SEE a car swirl to a stop beside some weed-grown field . . . if the occupants pile out with race-track binoculars on their chests . . . with cameras, note-books, and portable gun-rests . . . if they carry rifles (carefully as a trayful of Venetian glass) that are mounted with two-foot telescopic sights . . .

They are not, these unusual Nimrods, out for African elephant. Or alpine chamois.

They are just woodchuck hunters. And that, as a rule, is another way of saying a "rifle crank" — a man for whom the remodeling of a sporting arm for the special requirements of chuck hunting is a labor of love and an exercise in exquisite precision, indulged in all winter, perhaps, in anticipation of this day. They are not so much game hunters, strictly speaking, as expert marksmen; many of them are highly trained technical specialists, in other walks of life, for whom the nice calculation of velocity, windage, foot-poundage, and all the trig and math of range-finding and ballistics mean more than bringing home a rasher of groundhog. So they form a special class of sportsmen as distinctive as their weapons and ammunition (high velocity, low report, non-ricocheting), and like other specialists they sometimes differ sharply among themselves, but I don't advise you to argue with them if, like me, you are an outsider to their game.

Yet, however technical their jargon, however grim their expressions as they crawl to their posts, inch by inch, and cautiously bring their fearsome-looking arms to rest on the old snakerail fence, they are a harmless bunch. Except, of course, to the groundhogs, or woodchucks, over there in the thistle patch, lolling on their front porches and positively sunning their teeth — those white, white buck teeth — in grins of satisfaction that an all-wise Mother Nature should so provide chucks with that useful sower of clover and alfalfa, the farmer.

Let's throw ourselves down in the sorrel and curly dock, prone like the chuck hunters as they begin to pose their rifles on their gun-rests, their feet wide apart, their elbows digging into the ground like Army sharpshooters, peering down the barrels of their scopes. Raising binoculars, we too get a good close-up of the little creature who will never let you study him at short range unless he is dead or dying. He looks a bit like a badger, with that blunt nose and that grizzled hide; he certainly reminds you of a chipmunk, in the way he sticks his head out of his den, pulls it in, sticks it out again. He makes you think of a prairie dog as he sits up in front of his burrow, and if you should happen to see him digging in for dear life he will remind you of a mole. Actually he is a marmot — *Marmota monax* to the zoologists — and a marmot is a hibernating, subterranean relative of the squirrels, chipmunks, and gophers, with a clear bird-like whistle or metallic voice. From this we get his alias of "whistlepig."

In coloration the woodchuck differs somewhat in different parts of his wide range, which is from eastern Canada south to the southern Appalachians and west to the Missouri River and a bit beyond, and far across Canada, with an isolated subspecies in British Columbia. But, to speak generally of *Marmota monax,* he has a coat of a warm buff hue but with long black guardhairs that are tipped with silver. This gives him a grizzled or pepper-and-salt appearance, with the fat little belly paler, the blunt head dark, and the feet and ankles black, as if the little fellow wore black boots and black gloves. All-black woodchucks are fairly common, near-albinos fairly rare, but neither constitutes a different species or even subspecies; all are *Marmota monax.*

In our lenses Mister Chuck this afternoon is looking wondrous fat and sassy, a trencherman bloated with good living, and weighing, at a guess, nine or ten pounds for a well-fed male. Thirteen pounds is on record. Much of the weight is fat, especially in the fall open season just before he waddles off for a winter-long sleep. The fat serves the purpose of a store to last him while he naps for four to six months, in lieu of any laying-up of treasure like the squirrel's hoard. But this fat is also a shock absorber for the farm boy's ammunition. It is well known that you can pepper a groundhog with small caliber shot without killing him. That is one of several reasons why the real woodchuck hunters have demanded, and got from the arms companies, a special, heavy, woodchuck ammunition to fit their specialized groundhog guns. So no sportsmanlike chuck hunter will wound his fat game, but drop it cleanly.

In our lenses, the woodchuck looks bigger than he is; a ten-pound male will consist of about five inches of tail and eighteen inches of critter. That is not a very big target, actually, and this target seldom allows the marksman to close the range to seventy-five yards; in fact, at twice that distance, the chuck may, at the least suspicious movement, drop down his hole, the way a fireman slides down his pole. When that happens, there's a lot of air around the target! Hence the rifles with the telescopic sights.

If you wonder how any sort of game in most of our eastern states may legally be taken with rifles like these — single-shot, set-trigger Remingtons and Winchesters, .22–.25 bolt-action Springfields, Sporting Mausers, custom-built woodchuck guns and rebuilt military firearms — the answer is that the laws in many states make an exception for woodchuck hunters. This is not class leg islation, as you might think; it is really the woodchuck who is the exception, for he occupies an equivocal position in popular, in legal, and in scientific opinions. He is rated both as "vermin" and game.

For of the farmer's truck garden and clover field he makes his chuck wagon. He riddles the field with his chuck holes so that horses are apt to step in them and break a leg. He fouls up farm machinery with the mounds of dirt he chucks out of his den. With all this, he brings down on his head the epithet of vermin. I hasten to add my personal opinion that the word is a wrong one, and I think most biologists would agree with me. The fact that the farmer has complaints to make of some wild quadruped does not make it vermin, in the strict sense of the word. There is just as strong a case against deer, rabbits, and even squirrels, but no sportsman would permit you to call them vermin. But, in the past, some legislatures have so considered Mr. Chuck, and by implication at least, the bad name still sticks, since chuck hunters are allowed to use varmint rifles on him.

But the woodchuck is also rated as game, and rightly so. In the first place, his flesh is edible — and highly prized in many country districts, so that city chuck hunters frequently go about distributing their take in preference to lugging it back to town and their possibly scornful wives. Then, again, Chuck is a game little fighter, who will face one dog or a pack of them, if he cannot reach his hole in time, and fight it out where fate overtakes him. His incisor teeth are sharp as daggers, and many a dog has fled from his first encounter with a woodchuck and never renewed the experience. Finally the groundhog is gamy, as the sportsman sees matters — an animal with both guile and spunk, curiosity and high survival value. No wonder that sportsmen themselves, in many states, have advocated a closed, as well as an open, season on him. They think entirely too well of him to see him driven off the earth.

The country where groundhogs are hunted today is not the one in which Mr. Chuck was originally native. For our pioneering ancestors found the woodchuck in the woods — hence his name. Woodchucks lived in the woods because the whole country was wooded then, from the prairies to the ocean white with foam. Meadows in those days were mostly boggy and hence abhorred by a groundhog who does not like water on his pillow. What woodchucks ate in the forest I am not sure, but I know that the few times I have seen a woodsy woodchuck he was almost unrecognizably lean, rangy, and quick on his feet. Doubtless he was always, in his aboriginal state, scurrying for a living, and just as busily dodging forest predators.

Then came the Pilgrim Fathers, many of them from Dorsetshire where a "chuck" means a pig. And at once three momentous things began to happen in the life and times of *Marmota monax*. First he was given his popular names. Then he had clapped on him the legend of Groundhog Day — a transfer of superstition from the European badger as a weather prophet. And last and most important, the axes began to ring, the trees to fall. This was a phenomenon that never stopped until much of the virgin forest had been swept away and the plow passed where the lordly oaks and beeches stood. Then came the luscious crops. At that point all the smartest (or laziest) woodchucks chucked the woods for a fine healthy farm life, settling in sociably with the farmer from whom all groundhog blessings flow. Here Chuck remains, despite all efforts to drive him out, by dog, trap, and poison, despite even the horrible use of cyanide gas pumped down the chuck holes. With tooth and claw he holds his own, while his good wife determinedly outbreeds the chuck mortality rate.

This profound change of habitat has only slightly altered the external boundaries of the woodchuck's range; the great change has been in the kind of terrain inhabited. Woodchuck country today is farm country, with all that means of grasses winnowing in the summer wind — the clover, alfalfa and timothy of cultivated land, the tawny broomsedge and bronze Indiangrass, the fragrant melilot and harsh thistle of fallowed and abandoned land. Indeed, there are some who think that the little marmot has been a cause of farm abandonment. But this is open to question; farms are abandoned just as frequently outside the range of *Marmota monax;* for many factors may drive or lure the farmer from his land. But if, when he is gone, you find that the whistlepigs are stalking over the acres unchecked — is not this infestation as much a symptom as a cause?

Put it another way: the very parts of the country where groundhogs today are hogging so much of the ground are the ones where agriculture has always had to struggle with a stern and rock-bound Nature. Western New England, for instance, and York state east of the Hudson, are commonly classed by sportsmen as the happiest chuck-hunting grounds in the Union. But they are distinctly in second place, agriculturally. Time was — in Colonial days when every locality had to attempt self-sufficiency — that this was a wheat-producing region. Catherine Schuyler, wife of the American general, set fire to the ripening wheat around Schuylerville, New York, to keep it out of the hands of the redcoats and Hessians advancing under Burgoyne. But today competition with the deep loams of the Middle West has driven wheat farming almost out of the rocky upland pastures of the Berkshire-Green-Mountain-Adirondack-Catskill province. Instead the inhabitants have turned to dairying and hay-farming; to maple sugar production and paper mills, and to taking in summer boarders who come to worship at the shrines of the Revolution — Bennington and Fort Ann, Ticonderoga and Bemis Heights.

This region is woodchuck country *par excellence,* say those who know most about the groundhog. Here

— at Grand Gorge in the Catskills — the naturalist John Burroughs had his home, "Woodchuck Lodge," and trapped so many woodchucks he made a coat of the skins for himself. The proponents of chuck hunting in this region make no extravagant claims for it, like the "100 woodchucks a day" we hear of in Ontario. They do say that every day is Groundhog Day, save in the dead of winter, and that here Chuck has everything to his liking.

He likes the big field-rocks that have defied the farmers for centuries, for when he makes a home beneath them not even his arch enemy the red fox can dig him out easily. He likes the old stone walls piled up with such back-breaking toil by the farmer's ancestors. For they make grand summer hide-outs from dog and gun. He likes the fence-row thickets of sumac and poison ivy, bramble and choke cherry and juniper, for they give him sanctuary and provide him with berries. Above all he likes the orchards of the famed apple country in the upper Hudson and Champlain valleys. He camps out beneath their boughs, waiting for windfalls of the pearmains that look as if they were blue with the chill of frosty nights, the snow apples, red as holly berries outside and inwardly white as January, the olden golden russets like the colors of river mists at sunset, and the gillyflowers and twenty-ounces that the rest of the country may have forgotten, but that Vermont and York state still loyally grow.

And I guarantee that you too will like the woodchuck's favorite country — for its covered bridges and the cold crooked brooks beneath them, for the big barns where the cider is hardening in the stone-built cellars, and for the slicked-down look of its hay farms raked hard as the hair of a schoolboy in love. You will love its towns, shaded with ancient elms and maples, the frame houses drawn back from the street, every one without exception white-painted, green-shuttered. You will love the hills crowned with dark, pointed hemlocks. And most of all you will like the old-style Americanism, the upstate, durable core of independence keeping alive the spirit of Seventy-Seven when Dan Morgan's sharpshooters (woodchuck hunters, surely!) hunted redcoats and Hessians in the green till "Gentleman Johnny" Burgoyne had had to ground his arms. At Independence Hall, in Philadelphia, you can see the faded battle flags that our foes surrendered that seventeenth day of October at Saratoga. But the maples at Freeman's Farm and Stark's Knob (where Molly Stark *didn't* become a widow) remember the event each year and hang out the original American colors — scarlet and orange, crimson and gold, in a shout of triumph.

Now for the peace-loving animal citizen of this ancient battleground — he may not be handsome; his hide is rejected by the furriers; there is nothing especially beneficial about him. And some say he's stupid. But the last I deny. True that he is sleepy as a dormouse. That is because he hibernates for four or five months out of the year, or even more — for he often goes to bed while Indian Summer is still mild and food plentiful. Even in summer he sleeps all night and takes siestas in the daytime, when not prodded by some need into activity. But when awake he is nobody's fool.

Take his den, for instance. It is carefully provided with more than one exit — just in case of red fox, snake, weasel, skunk, farm dog, boy, or other act of God. And these back doors differ radically from the front one, which is usually large at the mouth, gradual in descent, and marked by a telltale mound of earth which the hunter spots from afar and on which the dog and all other predators can smell woodchuck paws and droppings unmistakably. The rear exits, on the contrary, are very small in diameter, hidden by grass or boulders; they have a mine-shaft descent and no tailings to give away their location. That is because they were dug from the inside up to the surface, all the excavated earth having been taken down through the den and out the front door. As a result, the hunter does not see them, the dogs don't flair them. And so they are not attacked or kept under surveillance by besiegers. A secret exit, of course, serves just as well for a secret entrance. Many a woodchuck, caught away from his front door by dogs, will back away, gritting his cheek teeth, gnashing his front ones, thrashing his tail and whistling bloody murder, till he can back up to one of his secret chuck holes whose locality he has had vividly in mind all the time. Then down he shoots, while the dogs bark, bay, snuffle, and ineffectually paw. Too late: Mr. Chuck took an express elevator to the basement floor. There he dashes by subway to the end of the line, where he waits for better times. Stupid, is he?

Generally the groundhog has the whole area dotted with digging and the front and back entrances thereto appertaining, and from them radiate a series of paths well beaten to the beans, peas, cantaloupe, corn, wheat, rye, barley, cabbage, and lettuce of the long-suffering farmer. Along these little highroads, which have been carefully planned and built with much secrecy, he can hustle, if retribution seems near. In extremity he will plunge down a neighbor's chuck hole, but if the owner is at home he will be hastened out again, with savage bites, even if the fugitive will go to the dogs if evicted. As a householder Chuck is inhospitable and surly. Outside his den, he is fairly sociable with others of his kind, claiming no feeding grounds as exclusively his own and always ready to befriend his brothers by sounding his little siren of alarm.

The times when chucks are either feeding, loafing or, one might almost say, sitting around the clubhouse together, offer the only chance for the sportsman to get a good squint at his little target, through that precious scope of his which adds up to two top-heavy pounds to the weight of his rifle, and up to one hundred and fifty per cent to its cost. And the amount of time that a woodchuck is actually in view is less in practice than it would seem to be in theory. For you almost never catch a groundhog out on a rainy or a cold gray day (contrary to the popular legend he *likes* to see his shadow, and is inclined to pop inside again if he cannot). But he equally shuns the middle of blazing summer days. What he really loves is the cool of the early morning, and the end of the afternoon. Chuck hunters know this, and concentrate on those hours throughout the open season. In general, that is in the autumn, when woodchucks are fat, when the young are big enough to fend for themselves, and just before the whole tribe toddles off to the long winter's nap.

We talk about the woodchuck's "winter sleep" but sleep is hardly the word. Sleeping animals, including the human one, retain their bodily temperatures unchanged, and their respiration and pulse, while quieter than in exercise, are not at all subnormal. A sleeping animal may often be easily roused; the farthest baying of the hounds will be followed by the twitching ears of the slumbering fox; you can rouse your dreaming dog by dangling a piece of meat before his nose. But there are hundreds of observed cases of the impossibility of rousing a hibernating woodchuck, even by methods crueller than I would care to describe, except by keeping him in a very warm room. For in hibernation the bodily temperature falls to that of the surrounding air and earth, if not lower; the pulse is too feeble to find, and the animal breathes only once in several minutes. A woodchuck in full hibernation in the ground is comparable to nothing so much as a seed — in which the life processes sink almost to the vanishing point. Yet all the power of the oak is potential in the acorn. And the day will come — (and *not,* usually, on Groundhog Day) when the slumbering powers of Mr. Chuck are stirred, and he comes blinking forth, his store of fat used up while he slept, to face a chill spring day, and a larder nearly bare.

And he has, if he is two years old or more, other concerns on his mind at this time. Indeed, he may even lose sleep over them — which means that they must be pretty important! So if ever you see a woodchuck strolling under the spring moon you will know that he is out courting. He follows his nose, running every interesting scent to ground. When he finds it fresh, he steps boldly into the lady's house. Half the time he gets his ears pinned back and his tail savagely bitten by a rival. When he at last acquires a mate, he may stick to her faithfully — as long, that is, as the season's sex hungers last. But he usually trots off during his mate's pregnancy, which lasts about four weeks.

The helpless, squirming, rather ugly piglets are born in the den. Their mother often nurses them in a sitting-up position, appealingly woman-like. She is kept busy changing if not their diapers then their beds, but in the end she house-breaks them successfully, for woodchucks have toilet facilities in their diggings —

little pits at the ends of long chambers, that can be kept pleasant by throwing on dirt. These are used in rainy weather; in fair, the dirt mound outside the house will do.

When the youngsters are weaned on bits of greenery brought in by the mother, they toddle out shakily to see the world. Soon they are digging earth — what else would a woodchuck chuck? — making themselves their first little houses. Often a single youngster will essay several holes before he makes a very good one. But by the time that he has to settle in to his first winter home he has become an educated chuck, who can dig like an Irishman in a potato field, is a bold vegetarian forager, and an artful dodger of his foes.

Many a hunter has he defied; many a shot has missed him. And sometimes, just to add insult to injury, he will, while the sportsman is swearing, or scratching his head at a miss, poke his blunt poll out again, grind his teeth in mockery, then pop back as the rifle is raised. We can just imagine the woodchuck chuckles that must be chortled then, down in the cockles of the chuck hole. His human friends — for he has as many as he has enemies — cannot but rejoice with him. For the woodchuck is at his old game of playing hard-to-get. And while he goes on like this he will never fail to keep the most expert riflemen up to mark, while saving himself for posterity.

WHITE–WINGED

DOVE COUNTRY

WHEN IT IS out of season for that leafy trout stream, that forest hunting ground, when your world has got too crowded and strident to live in one more day, turn southwest for a vacation that is different. Complete escape is nearer than you think — four to five days by motor from much of the Middle West, two days by train, overnight by plane. And you will never forget the first time you waken to morning in southern Arizona. You may think you have fallen asleep in a pigeon cote, but if by chance there are any domestic pigeons within hearing, theirs is but one dialect in this doves' Tower of Babel. For this is the breeding ground of the Mexican ground dove, of the dainty Inca dove, of the western mourning dove and, most important to naturalists and sportsmen alike, of the Sonora pigeon or white-winged dove, one of the gamiest and, until recently, one of the rarest of its family in the country.

Each with its own voice or call, these four species fill the dawn with a rolling of the R's, and a *woo-woo-*ing of sweet nothings. I know of no other place where a single family of birds (in this case the Columbidae, the pigeons of the zoologists) so dominates the air waves. I can only compare it to the concatenation of trills, croaks, and peeps from a frog pond in spring. One wonders at first whether this is a local phenome-non — a peculiarly dense concentration of Columbidae where you happen to be? Or whether the sound goes on for miles? It does. From within the city limits of Phoenix (bustling capital near the center of the state), south to the Mexican border, the clear airs of Arizona thrum with dove call.

Native Arizonans are of two minds about it all. One persuasion seems not to hear the sound at all, becom-ing, perhaps, so used to it that it ceases to register, as city dwellers no longer hear the roar of traffic. Those of the other mind consider it the most monotonous and doleful sound in the world. Not so your out-of-stater, like myself. To me it is the very voice of a landscape, like the thunder of waterfalls in Yosemite Valley, or the wind in the tops of Oregon's grand coniferous trees; even the memory of desert dove voices raises in mind that red and blue land, stretching away and away in world-without-end perspectives. Of all earthly scenery this is the most unearthly — indeed, it looks like a segment of some older and dryer planet, with its wind-sculptured minarets, its talus tumbled in seismic ruins, its river valleys without water, its vegetation clinging to the memory of silenced streams.

Yet, though so little like the rest of America, white-wing country is rich in associations of our heroic age. For this is "Old Army" country, old Apache and pueblo country, with names and memories to stir the heart like a bugle call and a war whoop — names of great frontier campaigners like Crook and Miles and Pershing, of grim warriors like Geronimo, Cochise, and Victorio. And here, four hundred years ago, came Coronado and his Spanish adventurers, toiling in medieval armor through the desert to find the fabled Seven Cities of Cibola. Here Father Kino came as one crying in the wilderness, gentling with his crucifix where the Dons had failed with the sword. And this is old stagecoach and holdup country, where "Curly Bill" and "Johnny-behind-the-deuce" played hide-and-seek with Sheriff Behan and United States Marshal Wyatt Earp. Dead-shots, the lot of them, and their targets were not doves!

Before you strike out into the desert, look around the ranches and the alfalfa fields, and you may make the acquaintance of two of the doves that account for much of the sweet racket you woke to. You will recognize the Mexican ground dove the moment it flies, for it seems to jerk itself through the air with effortful spurts. Its note is a long-drawn-out *woo-oo-oo,* uttered at short intervals, and to me it sounds quite ventriloquistic; I always think it is coming across a ten-acre field, when it may be but ten feet away. The Inca dove looks like a quail, all covered as it is with scale-like feathers, and so tame is it that I have seen it in city parks mincing prettily about like a street pigeon. In flight, its wings make a twittering sound, the two birds may lay their heads together sentimentally and flute their soft *coo-COOR!* It can't be said there is much sport in such tame creatures.

But go out in the grain fields and on the range lands, and you will meet a real game bird, the western mourning dove. It differs from the eastern form on technical and ornithological grounds, but to you and me it is the same bird, with the same arrow-straight flight. And whether flushed from the ground, or driven from its perch on the fence wires, it flies off bird by bird, never in unison like the white-winged doves.

If your eyes were closed, you would know the mourning dove by the whistling of his strong pinions. But a whitewing, after the two first flaps (which have a silken rustle like a street pigeon's) is air-borne and flies on without a sound. That alone would be enough to distinguish him, even though he does look a lot like a mourning dove — about the same size, same brownish upper parts, same pinky-buff underparts, same black dashes near the ears and on the sides of the neck. But you can tell the two apart in simple ways. The tail of the whitewing is rounded, that of the mourning dove long-pointed. And, true to his name, the white-winged dove has a white patch on his pinions. When they are folded, it is seen along the upper edge as a crescent slim as a little new moon; when the bird flies, it shows clear as a mocker's white patch. With his tail boldly banded with black and white, with richly black wing-coverts and quills, and glittering iridescence on the neck, he is a beauty, and wild as they come. Almost as wild, almost as fair, as the vanished passenger pigeon. And he will lead none of your tame ranch life, and have none of your human company, thank you. For him, the desert, the true, untamed desert, with all its harsh splendors, yes, and even its thirst and hungers and dangers.

And there he is now, basking contentedly atop a saguaro, that vegetable skyscraper, the giant cactus, whose great, waxen flowers are the floral symbol of the state of Arizona. Even as we glimpse him, he hovers over one of the ephemeral blossoms. What he does there — whether he catches insects or sups nectar — nobody could ever inform me. But the fruits, the great, scarlet-skinned, luscious fruits that the Indians call *pitahaya*, are his favorite food. Much of his life in Arizona is spent around this astounding cactus. And much of your time, too, you will be wandering its

groves, laughing aloud at its fantastic gestures and tor-
tured shapes, the laughter giving way to deep respect
and, in the end, to positive love of this great spiny
thing!

For the saguaro is the chief plant citizen of white-
winged dove country. Sometimes thirty or forty feet
tall, with enormous branches weighing hundreds of
pounds, it looks like a tree designed by someone who
had heard of, but never seen, a tree. With its upraised
arms and tall, peaked "head," it has a goblin look, made
more convincing by those woodpecker holes in the top
that may appear like eye-sockets. The woody tissues
of the saguaro, like bundles of bamboo fishing rods, are
so strong that for centuries Indians have used them in
house construction, and the Mexican population still
employs them as ceiling beams. Bleached in death,
they look like bones lying in the desert; it raises a thirst
just to see them.

Yet if white-winged country is desertic, it knows
downpour too. Rainfall and drought make an odd
pattern in Arizona. There is nothing like it anywhere
else. In California, the rain falls in winter only, in
New Mexico in summer. But in white-winged dove
country there are two dry seasons and two rainy ones.
And into them every living thing must fit its life history, from rancher to roadrunner.

In the first three months of the year comes the little
rainy season, when about three inches of gentle pre-

cipitation falls in the cool weather. This is followed by
the little dry season. And now the whitewings come
back from their winter homes in Mexico, not arriving
in a great flight like waterfowl, but more after the manner of song birds, by welcome infiltration, bird by bird.
As soon as the males are in force they gather in
bachelor clubs in the mesquite *bosques*. These are
thickets of a thorny deciduous tree of the same family
as our eastern locusts, but looking rather like some
crooked peach orchard, with a curse of mistletoe put
on it by the evil spirits of the desert — a tree with a
million leaflets, that, turning their edges to the noon
sun, contrive to give the weary wanderer no shade!

And here, when they are not fighting each other with
guttural outcries and harmless flappings, the whitewing
suitors join in splendid display flights. You will see a
whole colony rise out of the tops of the mesquite and
with full quick strokes gain altitude, and then, at thirty
or forty feet above the desert sands, they suddenly set
their wings and scale around in a great circle. Domestic pigeons do this, of course, and so do starlings
and, on occasions, grackles, swallows, swifts, sandpipers, and many another bird. But none are so grand
a sight as the Sonora pigeons, as the sportsman likes
to call them, when their white wing-patches flash in
the early morning light, with their pearly breasts softly
shining and the iridescent spots on their necks glittering. And then, as suddenly as they rose, all the flock

will return to the *bosques* and puff out their throats in song. They do not call in unison — indeed, it is every bird for himself — but the total effect is a single sound that can be heard a mile away.

Strangely, no two observers agree about this song — some call it a "labored cuckooing" and some put it down in English as "Who cooks for you?" Some say it's gruff, some say it's sweet, and some will have it like the hooting of an owl. It seems to me that this bird has two songs. One is gruff and burring and definitely hoot-owlish. Perhaps it could be suggested by the syllables *who-hoo, who-hoo-HOO.* The other begins softly, but ends on quite a ringing musical note. *Coo-karra-COO* might do for a transliteration. So sweet it is that down in the state of Sonora, Mexico, the whitewing is some-times caged for his song, and called *paloma cantador* — singing dove.

One by one, the bachelor clubs break up, as each male begins definitely to pursue a single mate. Like a small boy showing off in front of girls, the male struts, pouter-pigeon style, inflating his chest, puffing out his throat, and throwing upward his bright wings and the tail. He uses the tail as a Japanese courtier employs a ceremonial fan — flinging it open with a self-conscious pride to show its fine black and white markings, then snapping it shut with a sharp sound like a final word on the subject that is interesting him so much.

Now indeed all the desert birds are at their courting. The Bendire thrasher from cactus and mesquite
pours forth his song that is like a mocker's in general
pattern but far less showy, for your mocker always
sings for listeners, around human habitations, while
the thrasher is a solitary and, like the hermit thrush,
seems to sing only for his mate, harkening somewhere
in the bitter brush. The swift, sweet tones, slender
and liquid, pour shyly forth; then there is silence that
keeps you listening eagerly for the bird to begin again.
Now the phainopepla goes sailing over the scrub, steering himself like a magpie with his long tail, his green-
ish blue-black plumage gleaming with metallic high-
lights, his wild crest erect, his wing-patches so white
they look like windows in his plumage. Now the ver-
million flycatcher, gorgeous as a scarlet tanager but
plump and scarcely bigger than a sparrow, dashes from
the mesquite into the air to snap an insect and return
in a flash to his selfsame perch. Now the verdins,
those gill-sized titmice with yellow faces, having mated
early, are already building their big, thorny, barrel-
shaped nests. The tender passion is felt even by such
an absurd, scuttling tatterdemalion as the roadrunner,
that outsize, grounded cuckoo, and his mate will soon
be building her ragbag nest of the inner bark of cedar,
of feathers, of mesquite pods, manure chips, snake-
skins, and God and Nature know what else!

Even to the desert's vegetation the little dry season

brings a sudden ephemeral tenderness. The fierce mesquite relents and fumes into blossom — long slim
sprays of white bloom whose odor sweetens the wilderness. The bees come in swarms to make their finest
honey from its nectar. And now at last the saguaro
blooms. The first opening of the petals is at night, beginning about eight o'clock and continuing with slow
deliberation for three or four hours. When fully ex-
panded the bloom is two or three inches across and
looks strangely like a water lily but stranded on the
desert and raised on a tower of spines! Each bloom is
queen for a night, and a day; before the sun goes down
again it will have withered on its stalk.

Then, while the little dry season mounts to a hot cli-
max, and the fruits of the saguaro, big as goose eggs,
are ripening, the white-winged doves too are bringing
forth fruit in their season. The dull creamy eggs are
laid on a loose platform of sticks situated high in the
mesquite and just depressed enough to keep the eggs
from rolling out. There are two nestlings, unless a cow-
bird has foisted its brat upon them, but it is no home-
lier than the legitimate offspring of the doves, for
baby whitewings are practically black and covered
with long straggling down. They are fed at first on
"pigeon's milk," a sort of mush from the parent's crop,
and this suffices for several weeks, till the youngster
can flop about in the mesquite or finally jump, tumble,
or flap to the ground.

Like an egg split by a little bill, the big saguaro fruits split on the tree before they fall, exposing the pink pulp and black seeds that remind us of a miniature watermelon. So important is this fruit, the *pitahaya*, in the life of the Indians that the Papagos date their New Year from its ripening, and the Pimas call this time the saguaro harvest moon. Jam, syrup, and preserves are made from it; it is also sun-dried and candied in its own sugar content or fermented to a weak beer or a strong liquor. White men prefer their *pitahayas* raw, and for myself I think them delicious. The pulp has the crispness of a tender radish, is cool as a cucumber, almost as juicy as a melon, and the tiny, soft, nutritious seeds go right down without protest from your throat.

And so mad are the whitewings for the *pitahayas* that in season they eat little else. Their black bills are stained carmine by the pulp. What the doves and Indians do not get, the fierce desert ants soon carry off. Scarcely one seed in a million, it has been hazarded, ever escapes. And by the same token, the doves, who may mate again and yet again, probably do not raise to adulthood more than one and a half youngsters, on the average, per pair. Grackles and green jays rob the nests, blue-darter hawks and prowling coyotes catch the young on the ground.

The big rainy season, in July and August, is as necessary for sprouting the seeds of the saguaro and filling its great storage tanks as it is for replenishing the secret water holes of the desert where the whitewings come twice daily for a drink. For the big dry season that follows, from September to January, is the hardest of all on every desert dweller. A full-grown saguaro will contain nine or ten tons of water in its tissues, and well the rodents and rabbits know it. Frantic with thirst, they somehow insert their tender snouts among the fierce spines and set their chisel teeth into the rind. Once they pull away the first chunk, the other clusters of spines are easily undermined, and so the luscious vitals of the giant cactus are devoured. Sometimes these ponderous water towers are so gnawed that they topple in the first gust of wind.

The whitewings cannot, like the desert quail, live upon dew. They must have real water, at least once a day, and sixty miles, at their steady clip, is nothing for them to fly for it. In little flocks of five and six they leave the mesquite *bosques* in a stream at dawn and again in the late afternoon. And so the hunters have learned to wait for them at the water holes, well knowing the birds have to come. This sounds like easy shooting, but in practice it is limited to a few minutes each day, for the birds waste no time, and return to their roosts just after sunset. Roost shooting sounds profitable too — since there may be as many as seven hundred birds in a single thicket, but only at night are they so abundant, and by then shooting is illegal. "Walking up" the birds where they feed, in the dry season, in the stubble of grain fields, is the preferred hunting method at the present. But the doves are wary, and when one of them sees anything alarming, the whole flock rises as a single bird. Surely, you would think, a hunter could hit something in that mass, and he usually does. But no bird but the jack snipe has so zigzagging a flight. The hunter is apt to find himself surrounded by empty cartridge shells, with only one or two doves to show for his ammunition.

Time was, and not so long ago, when no laws protected the Sonora pigeon, and shooting him was deemed no more than doing the Lord's work. The ranchers (never call a man a farmer in Arizona) complained that the doves were committing enormous depredations on their grain, and they waged a war of extermination against the alleged culprit. The whitewings were baited with grain and potted on the ground; roosts were shot up at night by the beams of auto headlights. The breeding season, so far from bringing the birds the sanctuary accorded any game by sportsmen, was the best time to curb the nuisance, the ranchers claimed. Every water hole was covered by guns of men and boys. And every attempt to regulate the hunting was met by angry opposition.

I would not say how real or false were the accusations of damage done by these doves when they were plentiful, and you must pass your own judgment on the methods once used to kill them. The historical fact, though, is that this species nearly went the way of the extinct passenger pigeon. Then the migratory-bird treaty between the United States and Mexico was signed, and the Sonora pigeons, as migrants from over the border, came under federal regulation. The recovery of the whitewings is not yet impressive, probably because a lot of illegal hunting goes on in remote parts of the desert on both sides of the border. But saved the bird is, and thanks are due solely to the federal government and law-abiding hunters. These may find it irksome that the bag limit is still small, and the number of hours and days of legitimate shooting is yet so curtailed. But, however many pigeons they take or cannot take, their great reward would never be in terms of fowl on the spit. It would always be in the fascination of dove country itself, land of resonant dawns, of thorns that flower, of red cliffs turning old Indian faces unblinking to the sun.

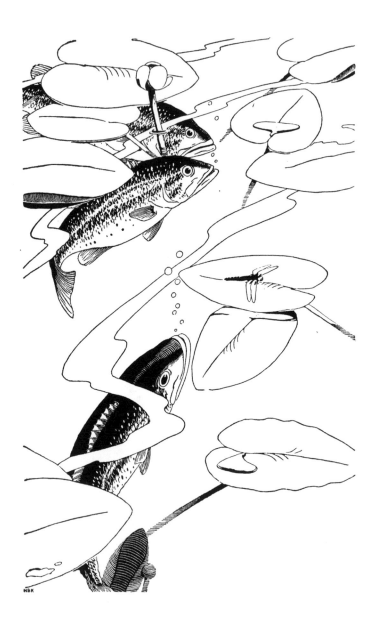

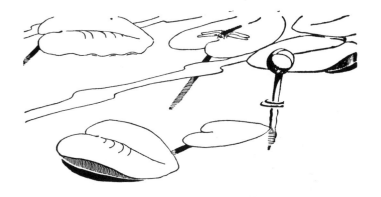

BASS COUNTRY

When a jeweler wishes to describe the worth of a precious gem, he compares it to water. "A diamond of the first water" is one perfectly pure and transparent; its luster and limpidity are those of the most beautiful lake waters. The lakes of this world, this old planet mother of ours, are her jewels. Rivers and oceans are not gem-like, but almost every lake is precious, worth more, a princely fortune more — in the eyes of anglers, duck hunters, conservationists, naturalists — than that same area were it drained and turned into the tallest corn that ever grew, or the thickest forest of oil derricks. Certainly any rodsman worthy of the name would, if he had the money that corn or oil might bring him, go buy himself a lake of the first water. At least, he will get a lot of good bass tackle, a stout boat,

107

a shore cottage to shelter those pumpkinseed and crappie fishermen, his wife and children, and give himself a month of Sundays to enjoy it all.

This lake world is a double world, half of it — the more exciting half — under water and unseen, save for a finny shadow, a silver splash, a string of bubbles. The other half is a wide arc of sky rimmed, perhaps, with cattail and bulrush, or, again, with fragrant spruce and twinkling aspen. Overhead the little black terns — the smallest, friendliest, and most inland of all the gull family — cut geometric patterns in the blue. The air is full of talk in the batrachian language — the croak of pond frogs, the piping of tree frogs, the trilling of tree toads, and the *basso profundo* of the old bulls. Immense as is the calm out on lake waters, it is stitched with the darting embroidery of those busy "darning needles," the dragonflies, that glitter even more intensely than the twinkling waters themselves. These fierce, fairy insects are hawking after flies, mating in air, or sowing the lake surface with their eggs. As on this errand the female dips low to the water, there rises a smart old fish to snap her from the air where she gleamed the instant before. And this, when you come to think of it, is no more than she deserved, for in her underwater days, her nymph stage, she caught many a tiny fish in her tigerish small maw.

The lakes of the land are necklaces through any region where they lie; the forces that have wrought

them are of many geologic sorts. You can have a lake
in the bottom of an old volcano crater, or an oxbow
lake made where a river has abandoned a loop in its
former course. There are those little lakes called cirques,
which are nothing but the melting of glacier ice
caught in a mountain cup. There are tropical lakes
forever warm, arctic lakes forever cold, and the brown-
water lakes in peat bogs. But all these are either so
distant that you and I will not likely get away to them,
or they are by their very nature poor fishing. And,
while I am about it, I will exclude the five Great Lakes,
which are inland seas, their shores swept by storms and
surf, their depths cold and dark; the Great Lakes are
for the commercial fishermen and the pier-sitter.

But the lake where you can hear all night the lisp-
ing, snipping snapping, gulping, bickering, and gurgling of finny feeders — that's the lake for fisherman's
luck. And it is a special sort. At least, any good fish
lake, whether you find it in Wisconsin or Finland, Florida or Sweden, resembles all the other good fish lakes
more than it differs from them. The best of these are
not usually the most scenic (obnoxious word!) for
the kind they show on travel posters are mountain
lakes; such are cup-shaped and their steep sides give
little hold to vegetation, while their blue transparency
betrays a lack of that precious ingredient in good fishing waters, the plankton, a soup of microscopic life,
which is a principle food of forage fishes.

No, the lake for your rod and reel is a saucer-shaped lake; its water is blue-green to green to yellow. These are what the scientists call eutrophic lakes — well-nourished is the meaning of the word. Sunlight can thrust its warm bright fingers down to most of the bottom. That bottom is mucky, rich in decay as a fine garden soil in humus. There should be a lot of shoal water, but a few deep holes as well. The whole body of the water should be big enough not to heat up excessively under the July sun, or to stay for long frozen deep and all over when January blows. The shores of such a lake make unexciting scenery, but that is not to say they have no beauty. It is of a tranquil sort, tranquil as the lisp of cottonwood leaves, the dappling of reflected light on the foliage of overhanging willows where the mayflies cling. It is sweet with the tinkle of redwing song and the day-long lap and chuckle of wavelets. The lake fisherman follows a philosopher's profession; patiently he rows and then, perhaps, anchors, casts and reels, systematically quartering weed patch and hidden hole. So he does not ask lacustrine scenery to be distractingly beautiful; and his family, also schooled to some philosophy, contents itself with the admirable safety of sunny shallows for swimming.

Such, then, is the upper half of bass country. The nether half is far the busier and more populous. The black bass and the rock bass, the bluegill, the perch, and the wall-eye, the sporting pike, the aristocratic lake trout, and the battling muskellunge are the privileged playboys of our lakes. They live only because a little world of other lives keeps them going. Volumes have been written on the gamy, temperamental basses, and you can find out — if you aren't already an expert able to tell others — all about the weight and length of rod, of leader and line and bob, all about the bait and lure, which will outwit the wily *Micropterus*. Far be it from an unsophisticated naturalist like myself to instruct veteran fishermen. But the business of a naturalist is with the pyramid of life, that layer on layer of the eating and the eaten, which supports as its peak capstone the well-loved sport fishes. So bass country literally goes deep; it is populous with many another citizen, each smaller than the last, in degrees descending to stuff so small that it strains right through the closest silken net and tests the last power of the compound microscope.

I have watched old anglers who seemed to be able to think like a bass, to know what he would do next or, more remarkable, to understand why he was doing nothing and where. And this, I suppose, is about as close as a human being who breathes with a nose, not gills, who walks around at the bottom of a sea of air, can get into bass country — its aqueous conditions, its finny psychology, its calm shot with ferocity, its green dusks and peril. The shores are easier to comprehend; shoal water has been compared by biologists to a meadow, with its underwater herbage of milfoil and pondweed, eelgrass and chalky stonewort; here dwell secretively untold numbers of minute animals multitudinous as the insects at the grass roots, and on this pasturage graze other creatures. Just as the wolf attacks the cropping sheep, so under water yet larger creatures are carnivorous upon those that browse; up, up rises the pyramid of life. But there is nothing in a meadow to compare with the depths of the lake — a place where the current never stirs, the light is dim at its brightest, the temperature may vary little more than that of a cave, and even for gills there is scant oxygen to refresh the blood stream. Here, close to the muck, the murk is deepest, the water stillest, the silt thickest; this is truly the underworld of the lake.

To understand how any creature can live there, we have to go down to the bottom of the question, and learn, for instance, that pike and carp can explore in such oxygen-deficient waters because their hemoglobin reaches the same saturation pressure at an oxygen pressure of two to three millimeters that a trout's blood does in the sweetly aerated waters of a dashing stream, where oxygen may stand at a pressure of eighteen millimeters. Further, pike and carp store oxygen in their swim bladders, like divers going down with a tank of it. Catfish, like suckers, have mouths especially adapted to feeding on the mucky bottom — lips that can be protruded, and the cat's whiskers help take the place of sight in that dim stratum, for they are really feelers, thickly set with sensitive nerve buds. The gills of the crawfish which live down there are deep set in the body and protected by special strainers that keep out the silt; the same is true of the gills of bottom-crawling dragonfly nymphs and mussels. The most abundant inhabitants of this thick gloom are the bloodworms — worms not at all, but the bright red larvae of the midges known to science as Chironomids. They cover themselves with tubes of mud on which collects their natural food — microscopic plants called diatoms; emerging from their tubes, they browse on these, until the day when they are ready to rise to the surface and take on the winged adult form, to enjoy whatever a midge can of the mating season.

Of all the hundreds of minute species that inhabit a lake, Chironomids are the most important fish food. There is probably not a fish, from the most playful minnow to the piratical gar hated by anglers, that does not eat bloodworms at some stage in its life. They devour the bloodworm eggs, they gulp the larvae themselves as these wriggle in their figure-of-eight locomotion, and doubtless the surface-feeding fish snap at adult midges incautious enough to approach the nether world that they have left. But the midges usually swarm high; what lake fisherman does not know the thin treble of their multiple humming? Toward dusk, especially, when the air is cool, when the fish bite best, when the children have ceased to splash in the shallows and the marsh wrens are settling down with a few last peaceful twitterings, the hymn of the midges fills all the darkening sky; there the singing cloud is invisible, but you know where it is by the flight of bat and nighthawk sweeping them up. To a Waltonian who knows his biology, midge music is sweet in the ears, for it is the sound of peace and plenty in the creel.

Smaller than the smallest gnat larva, multitudinous as the grains of the silt, are the members of that world-in-itself which biologists called the plankton, a host of animals and plants commingled which floats in upper and shoal water like a thickening of it. Plankton is to fish what grass is to man — it feeds much that feeds him. Only a few of the adult finny company, like the whitefish and alewife, are provided with plankton strainers in their mouths which enable them to feed directly upon this soupy provender. But most baby fish pass through a stage when they take it as young humans take the bottle.

The tiny organisms that compose it are the delights of the microscopist for their exquisitely symmetrical forms that, enlarged, look like fantasies in blown glass. They are the wonder of the biologist, for many of their plant members swim, or move rhythmically around, like animals, and many of their animal citizens contain chlorophyll, the green coloring matter of plants. The angler does not think much about them, until he notices strange discolorations that they cause in the water. One kind tinges it amber, another livid green, yet another a clear transparent green, and others still a cloudy green. Or, when other species become preponderant, the water may locally look like strong tea, or again, like soup too full of paprika. These hues are called the waterbloom — well named because they are a sort of flowering of the lake, as a prairie will be now purple with ironweed and blazing-star, and then in autumn turn gold with coreopsis and sunflower. Each plankton species has its "blooming" season. But in season and out, it is devoured by little water fleas, scuds, fairy shrimps, phantom Leptodoras, and those aquatic helicopters, the rotifers. Plankton is indeed the broad base of the lake's pyramid of life.

Everyone who has dropped a hook in lake waters knows that the fish are not found at the same depth at all times of day and night, in summer and in winter. They are not following whims, however; they are following the plankton and the next block above it, in the pyramid of life — the water fleas and fairy shrimps, scuds and rotifers and their like, just visible to the naked eye, or nearly so. For the plankton, and with it all the animal life in the lake, rises and falls with day and night, and with the great temperature overturns that come seasonally. This rhythmical cycle has been compared to the beating of an organism's heart; it is as essential to the plankton creatures' lives, and as involuntary. When one of them ceases to respond to the rhythm, it is dead; it sinks like a tiny vessel to add fertility to the rich bottom.

As little fishes grow to big ones, they get farther and farther from direct dependence on the minute life of the lake, and devour successively larger forage. Take, for instance, the pumpkinseed, whose rainbow flanks adorn the small boy's string of catch; when but one inch long, it lives on the smallest of midge larvae and water fleas. At two inches, it is eating half-grown bloodworms, nymphs of the smaller mayflies, and minute snails. Then the pumpkinseed becomes a big boy — three inches long; he eats the biggest midge and mayfly larvae, and caddis worms. But at the same time he has now become the favorite food of the voracious roving bullhead. It is the same with pike. When they are newly hatched, they go around picking up water fleas one by one with all the effort of a baby gathering crumbs, but they will end by snapping at the biggest frogs, and, among fishes, nothing smaller than a golden shiner will tempt their appetites.

Where are the fish? That's what we would all like to know as we cut bait. Perch and pike may have been in shoal water yesterday, but today they may be in the middle of the lake. But most of the sport fishes keep within zones fairly strictly defined. Just as you look for a nuthatch on a tree trunk, a canvasback swimming above eelgrass, and a marsh hawk over a rabbit

run, so you will find your fish where their own fishing
is good. There are mud minnows in one inch of water,
catfish feeding on the bottom from five to thirty feet
down — almost exactly the range of the pondweed.
Indeed, over the pondweed will be found almost all
the pan fish in the lake, perch and wall-eye, bass, sunfish, darter, and bluegill, as well as such predatory
species as grass pickerel and a large share of the forage
fish — silversides, shiners, dace, darters, and chubs.
That is why the anglers' boats, of a fine, cloudy, still
summer twilight, are to be seen, a miniature fishing
fleet, ten to thirty feet off shore. Fishermen are zoned
just as much as fish are. You will see only a few out in
mid-lake; they are after the gamy pike, most likely.

The bait in the boat bottoms is part of the story too,
of course. And, of all sorts of bait, mussels — used by
the long-cane pole fisherman after goggle-eyes, bluegills
and yellow perch — are the most astonishing chapters.
Burrowing shallowly through the mud or sand at the
bottom, or lying in the shelter of stones, these fresh-
water clams lead, as adults, but a dull existence, almost
static or shifting slowly on that "foot" which is the most
tempting part of them as bait. When they first hatch,
they are the most helpless baby creatures — techni-
cally larvae — in the lake jungle, and their lives are
consequently full of perils. In order to escape the suffocation of mud on the bottoms where they are
hatched, the young mussels attach themselves parasiti-

cally to the fins and gills of passing fishes. And little mussels know their ichthyology. The yellow sandshell mussel hitchhikes only on that torpedo, the gar; the lake mucket makes straight for the gills of bass and perch; the salamander mussel gets a ride with the mud-puppy (who is, of course, no true fish but a salamander hated for his fish-eating habits by all good anglers). As for the butterfly shell, it attaches itself to the sheeps-head, that pallid plebian drum whose ear-stones, roughly resembling the letter L, are collected by boys for lucky stones. As tit for tat, the sheepshead devours mussels, crushing them with the molar teeth in its throat; and the little bitterling is the fish that turns the tables completely by laying its eggs in the gills of mus-sels! Apparently the presence of mussel larvae in fish gills does their finny hosts no serious harm; when well-grown, they quietly drop off and begin to lead their dull, clammy lives.

Absorbed as the naturalist may become in this intri-cately interdependent life beneath the shining lake waters, to the sportsman with the tautening line all that he may be told about it leads, rightly, but to the prince of bass country, the big black bass. He's called also mossback, greenback, green trout, and by a dozen other cherishing names. He comes of the sunfish family — which by its very name declares its members illus-trious. So, for relatives, he has the smallmouth bass, the spotted and rock basses, the bluegills and crappies, the pumpkinseed, shellcracker, stumpknocker, and warmouth. But not one of them has the fighting heart of *Micropterus salmoides,* a showman, a strategist, vicious as an Apache when roused, stubborn as an ox, with pugnacity in the very thrust of his underjaw and sagacity in the amber iris of his staring eye. He varies, as fisherman know, much in color, but a few constant features set him off distinctly. There is always that median speckled line of black running the length of the flanks; the dorsal fin is so deeply lobed that it looks almost like two, and the maxillaries — that resemble the pouches of an old man's cheeks — extend back of the eye. A fish with the rugged kind of good looks that spell character!

That lovable, ugly mug of his is not the mouth of the finicking gourmet. You can tell at a glance that he is, instead, a Rabelaisian gourmandizer. He will strike (when he feels like it) at everything from bacon rind, night crawlers, and live minnows, to feathered minnows, plastic bugs, wet-fly streamers, and plugs of the floating, underwater, diving, and deep-diving persuasions. At night, he lunges at salt pork made to skitter in the weeds. By day he will take the flashing trolled spoon. And then again, in cold weather he is apt to sulk under a sunken snag, and perhaps those rising bubbles are his laughter at your fouled line.

The love-life of the black bass would be lawbreaking above waters; it is cold-blooded polygamy. In spring and early summer, the male sweeps away the silt in an ample circle on the lake bottom under a few feet of water. Then he poises there, in magnificent virility, until he has attracted a choice little harem. Dutifully the females deposit their eggs in the seraglio he has prepared for them; these he fertilizes. A single nest will hold from four thousand to eleven thousand eggs; over them the expectant father maintains a fighting attitude, driving off marauders — and the lake is full of such — and fanning them with his fins and tail to keep them free of silt and swept with a refreshing current of oxygen. In two or more days, depending on temperature, the eggs hatch; the small fry are almost anchored by the heavy yolk sac, and their first motions are awkward as a toddler's. When the yolk is absorbed they can swim enough to find microscopic provender. A few days more and these are on their own — in a perilous world of water.

Little bass are not precocious. By one year old they are but four inches long; on their third birthdays they measure somewhere around nine inches. A ten-inch bigmouth weighs about a half a pound. When full grown, the average black bass is a one- or two-pounder. The world's record, taken in Georgia, weighted twenty-two pounds and four ounces. But whatever his size, the black bass is every inch a king, lord of his country, prize of any creel.

MULE DEER COUNTRY

A GREAT DAY in the history of our native game was the meeting of those two gallant American sportsmen, Captain Meriwether Lewis, of the immortal Lewis and Clark expedition, and the mule deer, the grandest deer of North America. The place was on the eastern frontiers of mule deer country, near the Great Bend of the Missouri, probably in what is now Brule County, South Dakota. The time we know exactly from Lewis's diary; it was September 17, 1804. On that date, Lewis shot "a mule deer [which has] much larger ears than the common [eastern white-tailed] deer, and a tail almost without hair except at the end where there is a bunch of black hair."

Beside these mulish characteristics of ears and tail, the great explorer soon noted further distinguishing traits. Himself a Virginian, he was naturally familiar with the Virginia or eastern deer's antlers with their two snag-like branches pointing forward and giving off short tines, like twigs. But this new species, Lewis observed, had "two main prongs on each side [of the head] and forked equally." That is, each branch was double-forked to form four nearly equal tines on either side. Later, Lewis acknowledged the superior size of mule deer over eastern whitetails, after he had killed "a mule buck which was the largest deer of any kind we have ever seen, being nearly as large as a doe elk." Lewis might have become a famous naturalist, but his life in its early prime was cut short by violence. And not in the arms of one of those grizzlies he so fearlessly attacked on foot. He was found in the supposed civilization of Tennessee, fatally shot, and slashed with a knife.

Thus it fell to others to give the mule deer its scientific name of *Odocoileus hemionis,* and to complete the description of its surpassing dimensions. Records accepted by scientists show that an old buck of this species may weigh from three hundred and fifty to three hundred and eighty pounds after being bled and dressed. On the hoof a brute like that would tip the scales at something like four hundred and twenty to four hundred and fifty pounds of fighting flesh. The record antlers of this species are unsurpassed: thirty-five inches long, five inches in girth, eighteen inches from tip to tip, with the widest inside measurement twenty-one and three-quarters inches. Not even the Virginian deer quite equals this. True, the Virginians are slimmer and more graceful as, in full flight, they carry their white tails erect like waving banners, while the mule deer merely raises his tail in line with his spine. And those mulish ears, it must be confessed, are ludicrously out of proportion to the rest of the head. But probably you and I would be grateful for all the ear with which Providence in its wisdom could provide us, were we preyed upon, at all seasons, by the cougars, coyotes, and bears in mule deer country.

That country extends from the eastern base of the Rockies to the mountains of northern Mexico, and west to the coast in southern California. In so vast a domain, I shall choose as typical the Sierra Nevada mountains of California. For that is the place where I know mule deer best, and where the scientists have studied its requirements and migrations and cycles most intensively.

If you don't know the Sierra Nevada, it may mean to you nothing but one more western mountain range. If you do know it, you are already a fanatic on the subject; nobody who ever saw the Yosemite Valley with its waterfalls spilling from transverse hanging canyons, or the Bigtrees of Sequoia National Park, is anywise neutral about the Sierra. It is the sort of place we hope

to go to when we die, to hear forever the great plain
song of the forest as the mountain wind moves man-
fully in the boughs, to see forever the rainbows in the
falls, to breathe forever that dry, high, tingling, exciting air. The Sierra Nevada is the West as the vacation-
ist has always dreamed of it, the West that really looks
like the travel posters, the West of the white tent in
the flowering meadow ringed with the straightness of
lodgepole pines, a snowy peak rising majestic in the
background.

Golden trout are in that icy, slipping stream where
your horse stops to slather a drink while you lean back
in the big, creaking, western saddle, the sun warm on
the back of your neck. That silvery cascade of notes is
the song of the canyon wren, one of the most rapturous
bird songs in this world. That stumpy-tailed bird who
teeters and dips his knees is the dipper or water ouzel.
There he goes, right into the roaring torrent, walking
sure-footed on the bottom, and coming up with a caddisfly to carry to his children in that dome-shaped nest
fixed to the rock just above the lip of the flood. If there
is a better country for naturalists and sportsmen anywhere in the temperate zone, I do not know it. Yosemite National Park, which may be taken as typical
of all the Sierra, has eighty-two species of mammals.
On that roster are badgers and mink, mountain bea-
vers, fishers, wolverines; common big predators like
mountain lions and black bears, and smaller ones (and

more vicious), such as the bobcats and coyotes. Jack rabbits, snowshoe rabbits, and cottontails are plenty, Douglas squirrels, gray squirrels, whistling marmots, and chipmunks make wood and mountain meadow lively. But the king of game in the Sierra is the mule deer.

For this in his country and he knows it, with commingled pride and fear. And indeed wherever deer of any sort are found they are the most interesting creatures in the place. How spiritless, how fallen upon meager latter days are woods whence all the venison was driven long ago! But the mere knowledge that there are deer somewhere in a forest is enough to bring back the feeling of primeval abundance, of pioneering adventure. Photographers keep their cameras in readiness; children tiptoe, hoping to catch a glimpse of "Bambi." Naturalists watch for trees and shrubs that have been "horned" by bucks seeking to rub off the velvet from their new antlers. Sportsmen scan the ground, looking for "sign."

Of all deer sign the commonest and easiest to identify will be the shining black pile of droppings, so neat and dry and odorless, a find, when you come on it, welcome as nuggets. And if they are still warm and steaming, you are not five minutes from the living pride of the Sierra. Yes, there is a fresh track. See the spread of the hoofs, the incisive mark of the dew-claws — print of a deer in a hurry.

A sudden clatter of stones spurned from his feet as he leaps may be your first intimation that you have jumped a mule deer. For, waggling those mulish ears, he has heard you for some minutes, and grown alert. Lifting that wet black nose, that looks as inquisitive and friendly as a cocker spaniel's, he has caught your taint. The moment he sees you — off he goes, sailing over bushes four and six feet high, clearing twenty feet, horizontally, at a bound. Look, there's another — no, four of them — six — and a fawn!

Freeze in your tracks. Don't twitch a finger. They may stop, in that case, like statues, and turn their heads to study you. Curiosity and even friendliness is in their long, liquid gaze; if you speak, they waggle their ears as if to say, "How's that?" Now, indeed, with the sunlight shining through the velvet of their antlers like a pantheistic halo, with the fawn drawing shyly to its mother's side, the mule deer seem the incarnation of wilderness beauty. And all the dark wood behind them might have been created in its towering height, its dells of fern, its dripping staghorn lichens, but to serve them for shelter, bed, and board. As long as you stand still, so will they, in an innocent trance that might never break.

But try raising a gun, or even a camera. And off they bound again, smacking down on all four of those legs that look so reedy they must snap, but are more like steel springs that send the creature up again as if catapulted from the ground. By preference, mule deer will usually jump uphill. Perhaps they cannot go uphill as fast as down, but well they know they can travel upwards better than any dog. The canine pursuer will be winded in no time. But mule deer can scramble as sure as goats, and in a trice they will put the crest of the hill between their white rump-patches and the sights of your gun. A wily sportsman, a gallant sportsman is the mule deer, every thew and sinew of him, the finest game in all the vast domain he inhabits.

That bounding gait is something that the mule deer can only keep up for a half a mile. What he does next will depend on what he decided about you. If you were merely trying to take his picture, he'll settle down to a walk, and circle back to where you found him, for his daily range is probably not more than a mile square. But if you fired a shot (or slammed a car door, so that he thought you fired), he will bed down, panting, in the deepest, darkest thicket he can find, somewhere up near, but never right on, the crest of a ridge. There he can smell and hear pursuit, even the stealthiest, can bound over the crest if danger comes too near. Veteran deer stalkers know this, and never show themselves on the skyline, or expect to jump a deer by hunting up hill, but walk along just under the crest.

Still-hunters wait in passes where they know that deer on migration are accustomed to come, as their antlered ancestors did before them. For it is definitely established that there is a migration of the whole mule deer population in the Sierra Nevada. Their true home — where they are born, and where they mate — is in the great coniferous zone between four thousand and ten thousand feet altitude. Summer sees them wandering up into "wind timber," near the tree line, and even venturing out on alpine meadows. But the first hint of coming cold, or a falling barometer, or of snow in the air sends them down, and hunters who have studied mule deer longest say that it is generally a wise old doe who leads the way. Whoever leads, all come down in a hurry and spend the hunting and mating seasons, when the aspens are clapping golden hands for joy, at intermediate levels. Food is abundant here, and drink and shelter. But Sierra winters, the deer know, may be bitter. Some of the heaviest snowfalls on this continent occur right here. Drifts ten and fifteen, twenty and twenty-five feet high pile up among the Bigtrees and Sugar Pines. If coyotes ever work a deer out into that, they can skip over the light crust without breaking through, but the frantic deer, bounding on those sharp hooves, breaks right through; it doesn't take merciless fangs long, then, to do their work.

So that if a sudden heavy snowfall occurs in the hunting season, most of the deer will be found below the forest belt, in the chaparral or brushland. Here the hunter is visible every minute, his dog is soon hopelessly winded. But the bounding mule deer is as much at ease as Br'er Rabbit in the briar patch.

Perhaps that is why the sportsmen like the hunting season where it is — before the mating season. When that comes, in late November, the mule deer buck is an ugly customer. He has honed his antlers sharp as knives; his neck is engorged and stiff with the fury of his biological needs. His eye is blooded with jealousy. If he is a young buck he may run a doe continuously for days and nights, till Nature at last stops her in her tracks and she yields to him. The young bucks are inclined to stay faithful for that season. But the old ones are unabashed polygamists, wasting small time in panting after does, but herding them into their harems with highly pointed hints from their antlers. As all the does are not in heat together, a great many may pass through one buck's collection in a season, though only half a dozen might be present in his "yard" at a time.

And he could hardly keep more in order, for the young bucks come pestering and challenging. He turns to drive off one, clashes horns with him in resounding smacks, pushes him back with blazing eyes and angry grunts, downs him and makes him bleat for mercy. But while this is going on, his womenfolk are yielding to other young suitors. If the old man turns to punish such infidelity, then the challenger he has just defeated may return and cut a doe out of the yard and drive her exultantly into the forest. There is no moral law in mule deer mating except Nature's, and all she insists on is a fawn in every doe over two years old, or (much better, in the Dame's opinion) twins.

Now the proud antlers fall; now the buck forgets his jealousy, herds amicably with other males, suns himself lazily in bright clearings if the weather is cold, watches his loves of yesterday with indifferent eyes. Swaying with their great burdens, they step, with carefully balanced gait, down to the streams. There they try to slake the thirst that the fury of the mating season seems to rouse; there they satisfy a special craving for green willow such as they never feel save when pregnant.

Birth — say the few who ever came on a doe in labor — is not easy for mule deer womenfolk. They groan and bleat; they lick their new-born weakly, when their pain is over. But in a short time they are up on their dainty feet and right on their job as mothers. If you see a doe in spring grazing unconcernedly in the meadow grass, you may well suspect her fawns are near, but you will not likely see them. They are taught from the first to lie flat in the tall grass, their legs stretched out stiffly fore and aft, their bellies and chins to the ground. They are not to rise till called by a low whistling bleat. Twice a day, only, they are nursed, morning and evening. The rest of the time their mother keeps well away from them, never looks in their direction. She gazes at a human passerby with an expression of stupid innocence. "Fawn? What fawn? I haven't got any," she seems to say. "Haven't seen one around here for a year."

In sixty or seventy-five days, the mother weans her children. She does this, generally, by giving them the slip, leaving them, like the babes in the wood, to shift for themselves. At this time (late summer) many tourists pick up "lost fawns." They carry them home, in mistaken compassion, where too often they either die from wrong feeding or, becoming pets, are in some unwary moment set upon by hostile dogs or other predators. So those "lost" fawns are not lost; they are quite at home and if left alone will live to make more little fawns.

Are mule deer on the decrease, or are there not actually too many for their own good? You can get up an argument on these questions around any hunter's campfire, or in the offices of any game commission in the western states. If there is a pat and complete answer, I do not know it. Naturally the mule deer has been driven from much of the country once called his. Cattle, and, still more seriously, sheep, have been eating up the deer's browse on the western range lands for fifty and seventy-five years. For instance, in 1897 Ernest Thompson Seton saw three mule deer in the Badlands of the Little Missouri where, a decade before he had counted one hundred and sixty. And deer statistics stayed that way (or people assumed they did) until the story of the Kaibab deer broke in 1923.

The Kaibab Game Refuge, near the north rim of the Grand Canyon, was 754,600 acres set aside by that White House sportsman, Theodore Roosevelt. It was believed that there were three thousand deer in the forest at that time, but seventeen years later the number was estimated at twenty thousand, and a year later it was some thirty thousand — on a range fitted to support only half that number. The deer, having devoured every browse plant in the Kaibab, were found starving to death. And compared with the agonies of starvation, death in the jaws of a bobcat, cougar, or coyote is swift and merciful.

Blame for the Kaibab tragedy of success was laid by everybody interested on anybody but themselves. The forest rangers felt that the ranchmen, by insisting on extermination campaigns against coyotes and mountain lions, had removed the natural check on the deer. Some of the hunters insisted that the government was overprotecting the deer on the public lands, and that the hunting season should be lengthened or opened wide, and extended to include does. Their proposal to solve the Kaibab crisis by being allowed wholesale slaughter in a game sanctuary naturally met with blazing opposition from the conservationists. The Forest Service proposed to trap the surplus animals and send them to areas with depleted deer populations, but

Arizona state officials rushed to court, claiming ownership of the game. In the end the whole thing solved itself; by stern, cruel methods, Nature reduced the deer population; the browse and grazing grasses slowly recovered, and biologists, hunters, and rangers had all had a good lesson. Which none took to heart. There have been many "little Kaibabs" since and elsewhere, with the same generation of heat without light, the same old arguments and recriminations.

One of the ticklish situations right today (though it doesn't concern hunters directly), is the overcrowding and overtameness of deer on the floor of Yosemite Valley, where the herd has become one of the leading tourist attractions of the Park. Lured to the constant handouts of buns, cakes, chocolate bars, peanuts, sandwiches, lozenges and what-not, the deer have become so tame that even the fawns no longer hide but sidle up engagingly to get their share of unwholesome food. But the tameness of the fawns may conceal the fierce maternal instincts of the does. For the tourists, especially women and children, go into ecstasies over the winsome youngsters, caressing them and even trying to hug them and pick them up. Then at any moment a doe may take it into her mulish head that her pride and joy is about to be strangled or kidnapped. And an enraged doe is far more dangerous than a rutting buck, because no one suspects her. Yet in a flash she can bring those razor-sharp hooves down on an unwary human, cutting children's faces and women's breasts to ribbons. In vain, the Park authorities beg the tourists, by word and print, not to feed or caress the deer but to be content with photographing them. And the deer seem to understand there is no harm in those little black boxes and will pose as tirelessly as movie actresses.

But I prefer my deer wild. I would rather have one glimpse of a mule deer bounding away through the brush, than an hour with a forest monarch so fallen from his pride as to accept Popsicles from the hand of the hereditary foe. Rather than have him die of indigestion brought on by picnic scraps, I would rather that he died of a legal shot through his gamy heart, after many a free season of running the does and of fathering dappled fawns.

RED FOX COUNTRY

THERE WAS ONCE a Hoosier who moved to Kentucky and became so enamored of Blue Grass society — mint juleps, colonels, horse racing and all — that when tackled on the subject of his birthplace he would say, "I was not born, suh, in my native state."

By the same token, the American red fox was apparently not born — that is, did not originate — in the region which we like to think of as typically red fox country. That is, above all, the mellow, storied, gently rolling country which is Virginia and her neighbors. But among scientists, fox hunters, and naturalists like myself there is still discussion as to whence and how this most taunting of animals came trotting into that southland, his lips drawn back from his teeth in a grin, his brush waving insolently, his nose a-quiver with exciting indications.

There are those who think that the foxes of our eastern states are all descended from a few pairs introduced into the Chesapeake Bay region about 1730 by some prosperous tobacco planters who thought this new wilderness would be much improved by the fine old English sport of fox hunting. Yet our red fox is not the same as the British; not only do the scientists of today find him different, but I doubt that a few couples of foxes could so have multiplied and inherited Virginia earth. Others suppose, on the grounds of probability, that the American red fox and his British cousin crossed their strains in Virginia to produce a hybrid. And there are zoologists who make so many species out of North American red foxes that we soon lose the scent of our quarry.

I hold with those who think that we have but one species of red fox, and that a native, whose home in pre-Columbian times was apparently Canada and some of our western mountains. In the dark coniferous woods, where he played but a jackal's role next to the timber wolves, he was nothing but a second-rate predator, living on carrion of the kill, catching wood mice like a cat, and any cottontails, varying hares, grouse, and ptarmigan that were not too quick for him. He had never yet lived in the style to which he wished to become accustomed. If any "red jacket" had ever dreamed that men would one day kill off the wolves for him, thin out the timber, open up the country, and provide in it larders of overstuffed, flightless, unwary chickens, ducks, geese, turkeys, and guinea hens, his friends would have considered him a pitiable visionary. So, through a whole geologic phase, the fox in the woods was waiting for true red fox country to come into existence.

It came with the coming of the white man to our eastern deciduous forest belt. There were done all the things that the aforementioned visionary Reynard dreamed would create his Utopia. This well-stocked and well-groomed province was not completely carved out of primeval country before about the middle of the eighteenth century, and it is notable that until that time there are no records of any glimpse of a red fox brush in all the Old Dominion and thereabouts. The gray fox was always in the picture. He is an animal with shorter legs and shorter wind, hence more easily overtaken by the dogs. When that happens he will tree, like a 'possum or a cat, but the red fox goes to earth and knows a hundred places for doing it. If all you glimpse of a vanishing fox is his tail, you yet can distinguish the two, for the red fox has white on the end of his brush, where the gray is black-tipped. These two cousins have by now apportioned the countryside between them, Gray Brother taking to the swamps and the tall timber, and Red Jacket trotting in his black boots over the cleared land and the brushland, the land of poultry farms and horses and hounds.

And you can lay it down as a fair rule that any place a vixen ever littered is red fox country forever, until perchance it becomes part of a city. For no persecution has exterminated this breed, and the more he is run by dogs, the foxier he becomes at eluding them. So he is still king of that hilly, rustic realm, half cleared and half timbered, where the woods provide him with covert and ambush and plenty of cottontails, and where the soil is not too fertile. For he dearly loves lands abandoned by agriculture and grown up to tawny broomsedge so protectively concealing to his rascally hide. And there he goes a-mousing by moonlight, since he has never given up the traditions of his fine, sporting ancestors, and all sorts of rodents are in first or second place on every fox menu. For that foe of the farmer, the woodchuck, he has the highest esteem, graciously permitting it to dig plenty of burrows and dens — which he will occupy after devouring the waddling architect. This country of convenient earths should also be well watered to slake his notable thirst, and the choicest of it is intersected by rocky ridges, as is the piedmont of Virginia. Up on these crests Reynard loves to establish a lookout — also a listening post and clearing house of scents. Here, sprawled in pretended sleep or half-sleep (who knows which it is?) he is informed by his senses of all noteworthy county news in the valley below, and he likes to think, when his vixen is giving suck, that she is safe in a den somewhere up here under tons of rock where nobody can dig her out.

And such fox country, varying somewhat in tide-water, piedmont, and Blue Ridge, is the very "eye" of fox hunting in America; the British sportsman allows that it is the Leicestershire of the States, and that, it seems, is the highest compliment he can bestow. The oldest hunt clubs and organized foxhound packs in this country are in the region of the rivers that drain into Chesapeake Bay. When in the seventeenth century Robert Brooke came to Queen Ann County in Maryland to settle near his friend Lord Baltimore, he brought with him eight fox-hunting sons and daughters, twenty-eight grooms, kennel men, whippers-in, huntsmen, and other servants, together with blooded horses and a pack of hounds which has retained its distinctive blood and appearance to this day, so that the Brooke descendants hunt the Brooke hounds on ancestral acres still. Thus, organized fox hunting in America is almost as old as in England — for the sport over there did not come into flower until the stags and great forests were nearly gone.

No Virginian was ever a greater fox hunter than G. Washington, Esquire. We know that he cut "ridings" in Mount Vernon woods the better to keep the flying brush in view. Clad in his blue coat, red waistcoat, and velvet cap, mounted on Magnolia, his favorite Arab, he rode point-to-point, taking Virginia's stone walls and snakerail fences with a high heart, while before him belled Vulcan and Stately and the other hounds he bred so carefully. And after him came Billy Lee, his colored huntsman, riding on Chinkling and lustily winding his horn. That night George Washington would write it all up in his diary.

> *January 8, 1768. . . . Started a fox and run him four hours; took the hounds off at night.*
> *April 11, 1769. Went afox-hunting and took a fox alive after running him to a tree. Bro't him home.*
> *April 12. Chased the above fox for an hour and forty-five minutes when he treed again, after which we lost him.*

And so on, to the tune of one hundred and six entries on fox hunting in the book that the master of Mount Vernon entitled "Where and How My Time is Spent." Evidently he spent a very great deal of his leisure time fox hunting; but I find only ten references to deer, and the same for wildfowling.

And I think that George Washington would be happy to know that the old traditions of his favorite sport are kept up, with pedigreed hounds and pedigreed horses and pedigreed Virginians on them. In what in Washington's day was backwoods wilderness, the estates of fox hunters now join each other in a band, with the warmest mutual understanding between owners about the cardinal sin of barbed wire, the duty of receiving and feeding weary hound packs till their owners can be found, and the hospitable privilege of offering fresh mounts when the chase calls for them. In this hard-riding, openhanded, and leisured society, each hunt club may have its own habit and insignia; the famed Piedmont Hounds of Upperville, Virginia, for instance, boasts a double fox brush which has traditional references to a mythical quarry of the countryside which had two tails. Only, of course, you must never say "tails" to the "High Church" outfit of fox hunting. Indeed, there is a whole vocabulary — they say it takes years to master it — of this ritual. It would obviously be a dreadful thing to cry "Tally-ho!" when you mean "Yoicks!" And even such familiar words as "chop," "crash," "flash," "fault," and "pink" mean something other than they would seem to mean.

But for every American sportsman who dons a "pink" coat — the brightest of scarlets, of course — there are, right in Virginia and her neighbors, a hundred fox hunters who belong to the "Low Church" crowd, though their proud name for themselves is the "one-gallus hunters." And the style of hunting that they follow is well called hilltopping or moonlighting. Quite literally does it differ from the hunt-club style as the night from day. Obviously you couldn't go steeplechasing in the dark, and, further, the one-gallus hunter insists that the fox leaves much more scent at night. The hot southern sun soon licks it up, by day, but the

night dews retain it. And the stillness of the night brings
the cry of the hounds more clearly to the ears. For it
is by ear that the hilltoppers hunt. Their wealthy neighbors, so many of whom hunt chiefly for the joy of riding and jumping, can imagine no sport in it. But the
hilltopper, tucking a thumb under that gallus, toasting
the backs of his calves at a campfire, wouldn't change
places with the Master of the Meadowbrook Hounds
himself.

He and his fellow members of the meet, all in their
ordinary togs or worse, summoned by nothing more en-
graved and embossed than the telephone, have brought
each a hound or two to this gathering point on the
crest. These dogs are bred not like the "High Church"
hounds, to conform as good pack members, but as
rugged individuals each wise in his own nose, eloquent
with his own voice. And when they are unleashed
upon the quarry, it is they alone who pursue it, while
their masters, keeping ever a keen ear cocked, make
bets upon the outcome, while passing a convivial flask.
Each man knows the geography for three counties
around, and can say when the hunt is heading up Pan-
ther Cove, and when it will circle around through
Moccasin Gap. Hounds and fox, by long breeding and
evolution, are matched to a sportsmanlike equality of
wind and skill; both can run about a mile in two minutes, when fresh. So a chief object of the pack is to
turn the fox to the hilltop where the hunters are wait-

ing to make the kill or catch him in a bag. Or, if the fox goes to ground instead, the hounds will soon bay the news, when every man scrambles to his mule or nag and hastens down to dig out the quarry.

They say that if you ever get hilltopping in your blood, it is a fever. A mere naturalist myself, I have never caught it, but many is the night, in my childhood in the South, that I have lain awake, listening to the hounds, and I can still close my eyes and hear the grand music rolling up the mountainside out of those stout hearts and lusty lungs. It was not till I went to England, at the age of fifteen, that I first saw men in scarlet coats, on horses with "heads like a lady's and bottoms like a cook's," with trained hounds circling round them, waiting to be "cast" — a pack with a marvelous compactness and obedience, a twin-like identity in markings and build. But for "mouth" (tone), and "bottom" (stamina), for speed and initiative, give me the hilltopper's dawg, be he Blue Tick or Arkansas Traveler, July or Birdsong. And for cunning and courage, for a patriot's love of his earth and a commando's daredevil wiles, give me the red fox himself.

I shall defend him on every trait in his complex character and take on all chicken-loving challengers. Let me deal first with the worst charge — that the red fox is vermin, a pest and predator to be kept down for the sake of game birds as well as fowl. Bad as the name given this wild dog, statistical studies made of the stomach contents of foxes killed by hunters in Virginia, New York, and Wisconsin show that on the average poultry accounts for only twelve and a half per cent of red fox diet, and game birds not more than one per cent. But rabbits, rats, and mice, all so harmful to the farmer, total fifty-two and a half per cent of the menu. The rest of the bill-of-fare is made up of squirrels, fruit (only some of it orchard fruit and that probably windfallen), and insects. There is some evidence that sheep and pigs are eaten, but probably mostly as carrion. A fox is no wolf, and seldom tackles anything more than half its own weight.

So the place of the red fox in the animal economy is decidedly beneficial. Yet, save in a few places where really fox-wise sportsmen are numerous enough to influence the game laws, Reynard has less than no protection. He is poisoned, trapped, baited, and shot from ambush like a criminal. In some communities fox drives are organized, and as soon as the brushy-tailed population is rounded up, it is shot down by men and clubbed to death by women and children! No sportsman calls that sport. Yet the red fox is the sportingest animal we have. In proof, for instance, there is the well-authenticated case of a red fox who made so much better time over thinly crusted snow than the heavy hound after him that he stopped to sit up on a stump till his pursuer had almost caught up with him; then over the crust, like an autumn leaf driven by the gale, he would flee to the next stump and pause there again, with taunting tongue hanging.

A creature that can play tag with death is in a class by himself as a game animal. And the very object of his pursuit is different, since his flesh is inedible and marksmanship and weapons hardly figure in the chase. Other hunted animals are also swift in flight, alertly wary, clever at concealment, but the fox is himself a hunter and understands the stratagems and psychology of his pursuers. He is intelligent, as much so as the smartest dog, till we have made a metaphor of it. By intelligence I mean the ability to profit by experience and to foresee the results of actions.

Take the case of the fox who will sit down with the pack belling in the next field and lick his paws to free them of scent, then jump to a rail fence and run along it. Well he knows that when the dogs reach that spot they will be hopelessly "at fault." They will mill around, snuffle, and whine; for them the scent has simply gone up in the air. The honest hound is incapable of imagining the trick that has been played on him. Or see how, to rid himself of fleas, a fox has been known, on the testimony of some of our best naturalists, to carry a stick in his mouth into the water; slowly submerging, so that the fleas jump on to it, he at last lets the stick drift away, leaving these bloodthirsty pirates hopping mad and marooned.

The handsome red-pelted little creature is more particular about fleas than a dog, and in his den he is a scrupulous housekeeper. There are no droppings and no carcasses left about; all is clean and would be odor- less save for that scent of his which even humans can detect. As fox hunters know, every fox has his own odor, and to dogs and fellow foxes this is as distinctive as a name. As he is a good housekeeper, so the red fox is thrifty; he buries what he cannot eat, for another day, using the earth as a larder. There are well-attested cases, too, where a fox has employed the earth as a splint to mend a broken paw or leg, burying the mem- ber till it grew straight. In the known cases, these were pet foxes who could count on food coming to them — another proof of calm fox brains.

The fox is a good father. Though he is not tolerated by the vixen around home toward the end of her gesta- tion period of some fifty days, he does not go far away, but keeps vigil, leading off any hunt. When the litter is born — four to nine blind, lead-colored cubs — he provides the food. Probably he shares in the education of his offspring — all born with a high I.Q. And I sometimes think there are no more appealing furred babies in the world. Grown older, they pounce, whirl around, and chase their tails like kittens; they cuff and mock-bite and roll over each other like puppies. And then suddenly they line up and look as demure as chil- dren in a nursery school.

The world they face is one where they must live by their wits, cost what it may to the enemy. So, every so often, you'll hear the tale of how some wary old fox, if he really fears he is going to the dogs, will skip out across the thinnest ice of a river, trusting to his velocity to carry him to the opposite shore. But the pack, weighing ten times as much, breaks through and is swept under the ice by the current and drowned.

That night there will be rage in the hunt club and vows to "get that red devil." But he is not intimidated by threats. Curled up in some den with his brush keeping the tip of his nose warm, he is dreaming of further vulpine operations. He has discovered a new woodchuck apartment, perhaps, and is planning to make a business call on the inhabitant, with a view to establishing a long-term lease for himself. He has just recollected, also, that there is a farmer over in the next township on whom he has not paid a visit for a year; the farmer will have forgotten and hung his gun away, but the farm dog, with whom the fox carefully cultivated a friendship, may be trusted to remember. And there have been enticing hints upon the wintry airs, memory-provoking odors that stir longing in the dreamer. Tomorrow he will trace them to their source, sure that they will lead him to his mate of yesteryear or to some new love, a quick-footed, keen-eared, elusive vixen, sweet to run with for a season. But sufficient unto tomorrow are all these good things and their attendant dangers. And a man could be proud to confront his own days so boldly and calmly as this high-hearted little beast.

HAWK COUNTRY

ALL THE HIGH blue heaven that arches our continent is hawk country. There these bold navigators of the sky cruise endlessly, and little that creeps or bounds in marsh and meadow below is missed by that far, sharp gaze. Nothing makes our sky look so wide or so free as a hawk hung aloft there. I like them all for this sense of space they grant us, and for the remembrance of a lost savagery which they bring back. Some of them are pirates, to be sure, preying on the innocent and useful, but many are useful themselves, and sail that blue as vigilant for vermin as any revenue cutter for the lawless.

Yet all are targets. But to shoot may be to slaughter a friend of man. So that the whole province of the Buteonidae has become debatable ground. Good hawk or bad? It takes a keen eye to know, and certain information. That the naturalist has, and figures to

prove the truth of it. Yet still the barrel blazes in the hands of the hasty. My neighbor Giuseppe's wife, Jessie, is a remarkably good shot. But she never goes afield for quail or deer; she does her shooting from her front porch, and hawks — all hawks — are her sworn enemies. When she hears a certain squawk from her Plymouth Rocks that means a hawk overhead, she rushes out, grabs up her weapon, draws a bead on some slowly sailing, loudly whistling red-tailed hawk — and lets fly with the lead. The trophy is then nailed in triumph on the barn door.

Yet Jessie has killed a benefactor. The diet of a red-tailed hawk consists in fifty-five per cent rats and mice (with which Giuseppe's barn is swarming) and nineteen per cent insects and rabbits (which commit depredations on Jessie's lettuce and peas), with only six and three-tenths per cent poultry. But Jessie shakes her head at my statistics. "Every week," she says, "I'm a-lose my chickens. Mebbe two-three. Eggs too and baby chick. I got eyes in my head. I'm a-see them birds. I teach 'em!"

But her real enemy is, in truth, too smooth an operator to let Jessie see him at work. The wild things know and fear him. The other day I was up at Giuseppe's barn with my bird glasses, watching some cliff swallows. Suddenly every bird in the neighborhood either slipped to cover or froze. And there, skulking like a shadow through the trees, silent as a burglar, came the trim and handsome Cooper's hawk. In one bolt-like, stooping flight he swooped on a chick and made off with it. I hastened in to Jessie's house to denounce the culprit, but all hawks are bad hawks to Jessie, and she prefers to shoot the ones that are easy marks.

Many a good shot who knows his ducks one from another, at a distance far as he can see them in flight, never troubles to distinguish between the helpful hawks and the harmful. Who has not seen a dead hawk along a wire fence in the country, spread-eagled in hunter's triumph, intended for a grim lesson, perhaps, to the bird's brothers? In my experience, these are practically every one of them "mouse hawks," as the ornithologists call them — rough-legged, red-tailed, red-shouldered, or broad-winged. Sometimes a marsh hawk, too, gets his carcass nailed up, though his diet is only two and three-tenths per cent poultry and seven and two-tenths per cent game birds; the marsh hawks, like the mouse hawks, are big and slow flying — an easy target. But I have never yet seen a Cooper's hawk or goshawk punished for its depredations. They are the slick fellows, that get away. The others, in the language of gangsters, are the "fall guys" that "take the rap."

True that sometimes individual birds among the beneficial kinds of hawks will acquire an appetite for poultry that makes them relentless harriers and a prime nuisance around pheasant farms and quail preserves. Marsh hawks, for instance, sometimes become the hen hawks on western ranches. An occasional red-tailed hawk will make a specialty of chickens. Such anti-social individuals can be dealt with when they start committing their thefts. But the man — farmer or sportsman — who starts shooting every marsh hawk and redtail is killing off birds that make rats and mice twenty-three and fifty-five per cent, respectively, of their total diet. So that it is of economic importance to the country at large to learn to distinguish the hawks.

There are, to be sure, some thirty-two kinds of birds of prey (not all of them hawks) in North America north of Mexico. It might seem a lot to ask of a Nimrod to know them all. But such an effort would be unnecessary. A lot of them are mere strays from over the Mexican border or down from the arctic, noted only by ornithologists. At least, if you have seen a white gyrfalcon or a Mexican black hawk, you have seen more than I have! In the eastern United States the tally of hawks comes to eleven species. Only two of these make game birds and poultry as much as twenty per cent of their diet. Of these, the goshawk is not a very common winter visitant from Canada. That leaves only one common chicken hawk, the big blue darter, or Cooper's hawk.

Let us get to know this fellow. He is a little smaller than a crow, and *she* (for female Coopers are bigger than their mates) is crow-size or a bit more — eighteen to twenty inches from the short curved beak to the tail tip. Coopers are slim and trim compared with any other hawks; they look "slicker," more as if they kept their waistlines down or had not so much wool underwear. In perching they have a curious, ugly, sly look, hump-shouldered, with neck hanging and beady red eyes watching. When they fly they do not, like the beneficial kinds of hawks, go soaring up and up in wide circles, or shooting in a long glide on the wind while whistling boldly. Nor does the Cooper, like the duck hawk, put on tremendous bursts of speed or do sensational power dives. No, its flight is businesslike and performed in stolid silence. The bird flaps a few strokes, then glides, then flaps again, in a crow-like fashion.

The adult Cooper is called the blue darter because of the gray-blue on the back and tail and almost steel blue on the head. The tail has three darker bars on the gray-blue ground, and the very end of the tail is delicately banded with white. The white breast and leg feathers are handsomely barred with broken and wavy lines of cinnamon; the face is white around the beak, as is the throat, but the cheeks are soft light brown and so is the area around the ruby eyes. The immature bird has brown wings flecked with white, rather owl-like in effect; the light brown tail is barred with darker brown, and the head and underparts are white heavily speckled with thick broken rows of brown.

But the important thing is to be able to tell the Cooper from the innocent hawks when, gun in hand, you see it from beneath as it hangs in the sky. The Cooper has short round wings but a long slender tail. Most other hawks have either (*a*) short round wings *and* short broad tails or (*b*) long pointed wings *and* long slender tails. Only two other common eastern hawks have the Cooper's combination of short broad wings *but* long slim tail. One is the goshawk, a much bigger bird, twenty-two to twenty-four inches in overall length, almost as big as a horned owl; further, he differs from a Cooper in having a squared-off tail tip, not rounded. The other is the sharp-shinned hawk or small blue darter. He is much smaller than a Cooper — only some eleven inches long, the size of a bluejay, and poultry in his diet is only one-tenth of one per cent. Small song birds are his meat.

So, in the end, only the Cooper's hawk in the eastern states is a common menace to game birds and poultry. Its diet is ten per cent poultry, twelve per cent game birds, and fifty-five per cent small song birds. Its worst fault, to my mind, is the good it does *not* do. Only seventeen per cent of its food consists of rats and mice, compared with seventy-two per cent in the menu of the rough-legged hawk. Insects form but five and three-tenths per cent compared with the thirty-nine per cent of these pests found in the diet of the broad-winged hawk. The food of that friendly, beneficial species is only half of one per cent game birds, and almost thirty-one per cent snakes, while the Cooper's hawk doesn't touch reptiles or frogs.

Yet bounties have been offered in some states on just "hawks" — any and all hawks. The state game commission that pays five dollars for the carcass of one of the rodent- and insect-eating hawks has cost the taxpayer more than that sum. For scientists have calculated the value of one of the beneficial hawks at twenty dollars a year in depredations by rodents and locusts *not* committed. So that makes a dead loss to the community of at least twenty-five dollars for each beneficial hawk killed. Worst still, the rats and locusts that the shot hawk did not live to catch are left to breed and multiply. Thus the original loss is increased by square root over and over. And it all comes out of the taxpayer's pocketbook, not by means he can detect and stop, but in terms of increased costs for his food.

The bounty system has been tried in this country for several centuries. It has included Indian scalps. At one time, certain Loyalist agents in our Revolution offered the Indians bounties on American scalps and, if hair-raising stories are true, the Indian, when he set out to collect white scalps for bounty, did not care much about the political convictions of his source of revenue. He took Tory as well as Revolutionary hair when he could get it. It is just the same with hawk bounties. The kind of people who make a business of collecting bounties either do not know beneficial hawks from harmful, or they do not care. The same sometimes goes for the local officials, often the friends and neighbors of the bounty retrievers, who pay over the community's money. Bounty shooters soon learn how to make a racket of it, and demand that the list of bounty-producing animals be constantly widened. By no manner of means can this class of hunter be called sportsmen. They are in it for the money only. Exterminators they may be — though as such they could do more good by rat catching — but *not* sportsmen.

Yet what a sportsman the hawk is! The human hunter should certainly have admiration for another creature engaged in the same business and showing such splendid form and skill. Every outdoor man knows the common marsh hawk, which you may see coursing low along the fields, very tame so far as men are concerned but a true harrier of small mammals. One day while watching a marsh hawk pursue a rabbit, I was surprised at the languid actions of the bird; he seemed not to be trying to overtake his prey, but was just shepherding it along, tilting to one side or the other as the terrified mammal zigzagged down its runway. Then suddenly, sooner than the rabbit did, I saw its fate ahead of it. The creature was being driven right into the talons of the hawk's mate, who swooped in from the side, and carried off the cottontail — dead of the first blow.

Even the Cooper's hawk wrings reluctant admiration from us. One reliable writer describes the marvelous strategy and flying skill of a Cooper's hawk pursuing a quail as it winged for cover, almost on the ground. The quail, which was feinting at another course, tried to wheel suddenly and drop into the bushes, but the hawk had already divined this strategem, for it put on a tremendous burst of speed, at the same time turning completely over, and with its back almost skimming the ground it slid under the quail with its claws open, so that the quarry, just as it dropped for cover, dropped right into the talons.

Edward Forbush, in his classic on the *Birds of New England*, tells of a goshawk that pursued a hen into a farmhouse and seized it right on the kitchen floor in the presence of the farmer and his daughter. William Dawson in his monumental *Birds of California* pays a tribute to the prowess of the little prairie falcon: "It simply materializes out of the empty blue and picks up a gopher or a blackbird as quietly as you would pluck a flower. The approach has doubtless been nicely calculated. The thunderbolt, launched from the height of half a mile, has been checked every few hundred feet by a slight opening of the wings, that the falcon might gauge the caliber and the intent of the victim; and the final plunge has, therefore, the speed and accuracy of fate."

This little falcon can kill prey far larger and heavier than itself. Jack rabbits, for instance, are twice the weight of a prairie falcon, but it strikes them dead at one clean blow. It sweeps over a prairie-dog town so fast that one, at least, of the inhabitants always fails to make it underground in time. My friend Alfred Bailey, the Colorado naturalist, witnessed the snatching of a prairie-dog from the talons of a golden eagle by this daring little falcon.

But hawks are more than swift and dauntless hunters; like human sportsmen, they have a sense of play. I once witnessed a sham fight between a redtail and a common crow, with feints and glancing blows, like friendly fencers'. Redtails frequently spar with each other — screaming loudly and showing off their flying prowess. Pigeon hawks will dash into a flock of migrating shorebirds, scatter them right and left without touching one, let them regroup, and then scatter them again.

Duck hawks, those speed champions, will sometimes do the same, dashing in among swifts — themselves the fastest of our small birds. The duck hawk, of course, is our American representative of the European hunting falcon. It can drop like a plummet on massed flocks of migrating sandpipers, strike one dead, then turn, wheel, pass under the falling bird and capture it before the victim has reached the surface of the water. One aviator who knew his hawks recorded, in 1930, being overtaken and passed by a duck hawk, while the plane, a small one, was cruising at a hundred and seventy-five miles an hour. When a duck hawk launches itself from a cliff on a passing meal, it probably strikes at two hundred miles an hour.

That hawks migrate has been known from biblical

times, and though they migrate by day, they fly so high
the flock is seldom visible. I was a child the first time
I ever witnessed a migration of hawks, and I could not
say now what kind they were, nor how many. But I
shall never forget the thrill of those grand birds, sweeping in and out of the misty blue of the piedmont over
the Blue Ridge mountain where I stood, steering their
course, undeviating, for the north. Their shadows
passed over me; their shrill whistles blew down the sky
and were torn away by the sharp wind. No thunderous
flight of bombers in formation ever gave me the lift
under the heart that came to me at sight of those pow-
erful cruising birds of prey.

Well may they seek the higher airs! It is on record
that in one Minnesota town gunners brought down
three thousand hawks in one day. And these were
broadwings — the most beneficial insect-, reptile-, and
rodent-eaters in our entire bird fauna, who seldom even
touch song birds and never poultry!

In October, 1929, a Pennsylvania newspaper carried
the following item:

SPORTSMEN SHOOT MIGRATING HAWKS
KNOCK DOWN PESTS
FROM POINT OF VANTAGE IN BLUE MOUNTAINS
KILL 300 IN SINGLE DAY

*Chilled by early October winds, many thousand
hawks are sweeping past the mountain pinnacle within
ten miles of Pottsville, inviting extermination, a chal-
lenge that has been accepted by local sportsmen and*

hunters . . . Impressed with the unusual opportunity
to wipe out thousands of enemies of bird and game
life in the State, Mr. C. R. [a local ammunition mer-
chant] today urged local hunters to co-operate in kill-
ing hawks.

That slaughter took place on Kittany Ridge. Within
three years that very spot had become a hawk haven.
A group who understood the economic value of these
birds bought a portion of the summit of the ridge and
established it as Hawk Mountain Sanctuary — the first
ever set up in the interests of the birds of prey. Not
a gun pops at Hawk Mountain Sanctuary, as the broadwings sweep grandly over the barren crag, sometimes
two thousand strong, but hundreds of glasses of sportsmen and ornithologists are trained in awe upon the
magnificent spectacle. The splendid roughleg is there
too, and the red-shouldered, the red-tailed, the little
sharp-shinned. The rare white gyrfalcon and the black
gyrfalcon have each a few records at Hawk Mountain.
The duck hawk puts in a fairly regular appearance and
the golden eagle, a very monarch of the skies, shows a
census of about fifty individuals a year on Kittany. The
American bald eagle is even commoner, and the fish
hawk or osprey more abundant still. Here is hawk
country at its primordial best!

Even Cooper hawks and goshawks are given sanctuary at Hawk Mountain — as they should be if
sanctuary is to mean anything. Let the farmer kill

them in the poultry yard — if he can. For this much can be said of any and all hawks; that whatever depredations even the worst of them commit on quail, ducks, and other game birds, they take their toll, of necessity, of the weakest birds. Thus the stronger survivors carry on the race, and the whole health and tone of the breed is lifted.

There is no use, and much harm, in trying to help Mother Nature by eliminating predators; they too have their place in the wild. Where game is to be raised in a small concentrated area, hawks can be wired out, just as a poultry run can be covered with chicken wire.

So, when the shadow of a hawk steals over your path, don't raise your sights on it. It is the shadow of a friend — a friend of the farmer and thus, indirectly, of your pocketbook. It is a fellow sportsman, one without a gun, one who has to overtake what it kills by its own speed and cunning. The hawk — with no more exceptions than we find among human beings — is an admirable fellow citizen, a sporting American to be saluted not with lead but with admiration, as it spirals up and up on the wind, uttering its wild war cry.

MARSH

COUNTRY

EACH SMALL MARSH, lost in the woods, or hidden in some oxbow bend of a river, is a little secret. Each great marsh, stretching away and away over the prairie or following a long line of dunes, is a big secret. Big or little, remote in the Canadian wilds or creeping close to cities, a marsh is the least-known environment in all the countryside where it occurs. Nobody but sportsmen and trappers ever go there. Nobody, that is, except the naturalist.

I love a marsh for its great arc of sky, unblemished with city smoke or country dust. I love it for the re-

served elegance of reed and rush and flag, for the awkward dignity of its birds. I love it for its comedy — the plopping frogs, the ponderous turtles, the sly joke of bitterns, the queer mechanical cries of its inhabitants. I love it for its silences, and for its sounds — the wind that whistles softly in the long stems and culms, the clicking of dragonflies, the soft slap-slap on the boat bottom, and the sudden songs that spangle the air in nesting time. I love it for the grace of water and weed and reed in motion together, for the long, reverent down-bowing of rush and flag before the lordly wind. I love it for its loneliness, its mystery.

Any naturalist may well wish he had half the sportsman's experience in observing marsh life — those long waits in the reeds, when the mysterious cries of bird and frog ring out, when even the rails cautiously show themselves, and a little wake of water may represent the periscope of a muskrat submarine. Yet the scientists may have something to contribute to this, and as is their way, they begin by systematizing the marsh and its worlds. They divide it into three superficial zones — the deep open water, the zone of submerged vegetation, and the true marsh, with its emergent stems of bulrush, reed, and cattail. Or, put in terms of behavior of living things, these are respectively the World of Swimming and Skimming, the World of Drifting and Diving, and the World of Wading and Hiding.

In the World of Swimming and Skimming, you find

the black bass, pumpkinseed, bluegill, perch, and blunt-nosed minnow. Above these pond fish swim the ducks and geese, and above the wild fowl skim the swallows, the swallow-like black terns, and the gleaming dragonflies. This is the world of open air, open water, where the marsh becomes pond, or lake, or river. It is the fisherman's world, more breeze-swept, less secret than the inshore marsh.

The World of Drifting and Diving is intermediate; its waters are shallows; it is the frog zone, the turtle zone. Any floating log may show you a turtle basking on it — a musk, painted, soft-shelled, snapper, or geographic turtle. Any lily pad may be a frog's hunting blind; there he sits waiting for aquatic insects to flit by and be gobbled up. In spring this is his balcony for serenading, and his throat swells out with soft, protracted song until he is more throat than frog. Here the diving beetles hunt ferociously; before they submerge, they open their hard wing cases and take in a supply of air which they carry down with them among the tapegrass, the water crowfoot, the duckweed, the pondweed, the water lilies. All these plants are either drifting rootlessly or, if rooted, then their leaves and flowers merely float at the surface; no stems emerge erect, and when you pull these plants out of the water, they collapse limply. Of this betwixt-and-between zone of the marsh, the pre-eminent bird is the pied-billed grebe, called — for his sudden and complete vanishings

— the hell-diver. But he hasn't gone to hell; he has come up there, behind your back. The gleam in his little red eye seems mocking. He knows he is no meat for the hunter; yet few save hunters ever see these usually solitary birds in a raft of a hundred or two hundred.

To find the grebe's nest of water-soaked rotting vegetation which floats among the reeds or is built up like an island from the bottom in shallow water, hunter and naturalist alike must go further inshore, into the shoalest water of all, the zone of the cattails and bulrushes, the wild rice and the wild reed, the World of Wading and Hiding. It is called so for reasons which do not need to be explained to the sportsman, since he spends a great deal of time hiding there himself. He can tell us that there is nothing more thoroughly concealing than the millions of slim stems and the flattened leaves which compose the emergent vegetation of a great marsh; when you look through it you cannot see anything moving ten feet deep in it. No wonder that the blue peter (purple gallinule to the ornithologist) nests here, laying the eggs on a platform of reed stalks built on rushes over the water. Here too is the secret dwelling of the mud hen, or coot — a bird ideally adapted, with those leaf-like green feet, for a life that is always half swimming, half wading. All hunters know the bobbing motion of the coot on the water, and the way when startled it half flies, half runs, upon the surface, leaving a long wake and breaking, as it hits the air, into a high cackle that can be heard a mile away. There is no better tip-off than the clamor of the coot, that some other duck hunter, be it human or hawk, is abroad in the marshes.

Coots and gallinules belong to the family of the rails, and these are the slyest hiders and waders in the marsh. When we look right at them, we still do not see them; when we hear them we mistake them for something else — for the *put-put-put* of a motorboat, or the creaking of an oar in an oarlock. And the rail is a ventriloquist — you can tell neither from which tuft of rushes he is calling nor how many of him there are. The only way that I have ever succeeded in seeing rails is by staying still a long time in the same place, but when a rail knows you are looking at him he may take one step back — and vanish, as if he turned into a cattail stem before your very eyes.

The little black rail is just about as easy to see as a mouse in a haystack. No bigger than a sparrow, its chicks are nothing but tiny black balls of fluff. The sora rail is a bit bigger, but so dull the plumage, so absolutely frozen the attitude when concealing itself in plain sight, that a sora may hide itself in three wisps of grass. Its cries, all around you, pass for the sound of tree frogs; sportsmen tell me that only with dogs can the sora be hunted.

If the cattails of an early May morning or a cloudy twilight seem to be full of grunting pigs, that sound

will be the Virginia rail, and if you are quiet enough
you may see it, stepping with a self-conscious dignity,
wagging its stumpy tail, and prodding the ooze with
its bill. The king rail is my favorite. Big brother of
the whole family, handsome in plumage, bold in behavior, it is a bird of the Middle Western sloughs and
was first discovered by none other than John James
Audubon himself. Yet for me too came the thrill of
discovery the first time I saw, across a slough in a mud
bank of cattails and willows, a fine cock rail with sun-
set-colored breast, walking deliberately out in full sight
of me, pacing with the heaviest casualness, stopping
to prod the mud, then eyeing me carefully, to be sure
that I was looking at him. I realized that while this
gaudy male was enticing me to watch him, he was dis-
tracting my attention from his precious secrets. I
turned my head sharply, and, sure enough, on my side
of the slough the female was hurrying her tiny black
chicks in Indian file for concealment.

The only bird that can conceal itself in the marsh
more thoroughly than the rail is the bittern, and I have
never yet succeeded in surprising a bittern in a re-
laxed and natural attitude. However softly I have
waded or poled, the bittern has always seen me first,
and, immobilizing himself with upthrust bill, turned
into an old fence post, a leafless pussy willow, a withered cattail. So that the first I knew of it has been that
melancholy or disgusted cry of *faugh!* given as the

bird comes to life and flaps wearily away over the tops of the rice grass. This is his alarm cry, but he has another call, heard often from deep in the marsh, that has earned him the vivid country names of "stake-driver" and "thunder-pump."

And, jeweling all this outer zone of the marsh, are the little birds that are not marsh birds at all, strictly speaking, but land birds, song birds, perching birds, who never go near the water though they build their summer cottages over it. Hovering on trembling wings, shooting up as if on the summer breeze, or diving down into the bulrushes like zooming planes, the red-wing blackbirds fill the air with their antics and their music — that delicious gurgling, chuckling song, half metallic and half liquid. If you pass close to their nests they scold you, but as soon as you show you mean them no harm they go back to singing their glees, rondelays and catches. Marsh wrens do not take your presence so calmly. As you come near their little secret dome-shaped cradles, the males bounce out their front gates — the tip of some sedgy growth — and jump up and down with excitement, as they threaten you with cackling notes. All the while their neighbors pour out rippling music. Sometimes it seems as though joy exploded inside them and a whole flock will shoot up from the marsh grasses on the wings of song and then subside again in a last tinkle.

Beneath these sunny, song-filled waters goes on a

life of a very different sort — a night life, chiefly, a subway life, a submarine life, belonging to the marsh quadrupeds. Only one kind, the muskrat, has (in the eastern states) been able to survive the encroachments of civilization. This is astonishing, when we remember the muskrat is the most trapped fur-bearing animal in our country. He, or rather she, keeps ahead of the game by typical rat fertility, as well as by the lucky chance that man has killed off most muskrat enemies, and, above all, by remarkable adaptability. Muskrats will live in any old marsh, undaunted by the near presence of man. Because they are so largely nocturnal, most of us have little idea how thick is the muskrat population, in any region with standing water, but I have seen them abroad in daylight, the nose and bright eyes plowing quietly along, leaving a triangular wake in the marsh's backwater. Expert swimmers, they swim in what would seem to be the hardest way, kicking alternately with the hind feet and holding the front paws up under their chins. When a muskrat submerges, so the mammalogists tell us, he stoppers the nostrils with a big bubble of air. This keeps water out of the lungs, but even so it is astounding how a muskrat can hold the breath for those long dives that will bring him up inside of his lodge of cattails, in the middle of the marsh. In winter, when the marsh is locked in ice, the muskrat lives in a house in the bank; it has an air chimney, or rear door, coming up on solid ground. But this little householder's favorite room is his root cellar. Such subterranean passageways, dug under the mud, take him to feed on the tubers and starchy roots of water lily and arrowhead and indeed almost every plant which grows in the marsh.

The plants, too, of our third zone, are waders and hiders, standing, heron-fashion, deep in the mud yet high above water. Perhaps one cannot say that any plant is really hiding from us, but the smaller ones, the fair blue pickerel-weed, the white-flowering arrowhead, the rosy water-smartweed are hidden by the great plants of the marsh. Of these the greatest, in size, in fertility, in world-wide distribution, in ancient geologic lineage is, I think, the cattail. There is no continent on which the cattail does not grow, and scarcely a marsh in tropic or temperate zone where it is not abundant. It must have hundreds of names in the languages of the world, and perhaps hundreds of uses. The Indians of Illinois had more than there is time to tell; one is suggested by their name for it — "down-for-baby's-bed." Graphic, too, is another name: "it-flies-around."

It certainly does; great marshes like the Cayuga must produce incalculable millions of cattail paratrooper seeds. But the rootstocks, down in the mud, are just as effective in making cattail one of the dominant plants of the world today. Intricately matted, hard as iron, they smother out everything else and advance into the marsh many feet a year, if conditions are favorable.

If you see a plant that looks like a delicate sort of corn growing in water, it is wild rice, not related to cultivated rice except that both are grasses and cereal crops, but just as important to the red man as oriental rice to the yellow. Some of the finest stands of wild rice left in this country today are within Indian reservations. To the Menominees of Wisconsin the wild rice is a sacred plant; it enters into their religion, a gift from Manitou himself, and the Menominees will not sell more wild rice than represents their surplus. That is one of the factors that puts so high a price on this incomparable accompaniment to roast wild duck. Also all hand labor comes high, even among Indians, and only by hand can this grand old cereal of the marshes be gathered. The Indians pole their way up the inlets and beat the grains of the ripe and bending wild rice into their boat bottoms.

There are just as fair flowers in the marsh as on the land — not so many kinds, but often larger and stranger. Marsh mallows big as hollyhocks, water lilies lovely as nymphs, cow lilies like butterballs could compete in any contest for beauty. But the lotus is the queen of them all. Our American lotus has yellow flowers, while the oriental has pink; both have a drugging fragrance; both lift their great blue-green umbrella leaves high out of water; and both, when their

pods are old, invert them, so that the heavy seeds drop
out through the pod's curious perforations. Wondrous
tales are told of the longevity of these seeds, and it has
been claimed that some, found in the beds of lakes in
China declared dry for two thousand years, have
proved viable. The flaw in this story is that the length
of time the lakes have been dry is guesswork or tradi-
tion. But scientists are quite sure that a few seeds out
of many might be viable after a couple of centuries.
This is enough to break all records, and is in poignant
contrast to the ephemeral flower which, though so
large and serene, lasts but three or four days, then
drops its petals on the indifferent waters.

You and I who love the marshes need no arguments
or statistics in their favor. But lucky the marsh that
has not vigorous enemies to drain it, fill it, or smother
it in oil. There are a lot of reasons for destroying a
marsh, some well founded and many more sadly short-
sighted. If a marsh is a genuine nuisance, it is bound to
go, but I believe that there are few cases where a
marsh is a liability, or can be successfully converted
into something else. For instance, the bad reputation
of the New Jersey and Delaware marshes seemed at
one time to justify a tremendous expenditure of money
to try to drain them. But in too many instances the attempt, owning to the lay of the land and water, was
doomed to failure, and it was the money that was
drained away. True, the marshes, as a habitat where

muskrat and duck could live, were ruined, but no good land was made, and the mosquito problem remains because the cost of keeping the ditches open is so great that efforts have had to be abandoned, and thousands of miles of stagnant pools result.

The Kankakee marshes of Indiana were some of the grandest in the country, famous with sportsmen for inexhaustible wildlife. Ill-advised "reclamation" has ruined them; and, though some rich farms have been built up where once the otter lived, many have been abandoned and become tax-delinquent land on the counties' hands. The Horicon marshes in Wisconsin, the Malheur marshes in Oregon are classic examples of mismanagement for what were probably high moral motives. Since the days of the Roman emperors, it has been supposed to be a contribution to humanity to drain a marsh, and this might well be so in malarial countries. In the northern United States, surely, it is throwing away a unique asset, whether we are talking about the vast Montezuma marshes of New York state or two acres of water crowfoot and bulrush on an Iowa farm, where the cattle can get drink that the farmer does not have to pump or carry, and where a migrating duck can find a resting place.

At least as wise as the Roman emperor who drained a marsh was the Egyptian king who made one, creating a vast shallow with waters diverted from the Nile, and so affording a breeding ground for storks and cranes, teal and ducks. For a marsh is one kind of wilderness which *can* be restored. Impounded shallow waters will quickly fill up with the typical marsh plants, and where they grow the marsh animals gladly troop or swim or flock. The United States Biological Survey, for instance, has for years had a policy of restoring as well as protecting marshes. It has done a magnificent job, which could be better if it were not hampered by lack of funds. Those funds come from Congress, and perhaps most Congressmen find it easier to go to their constituents with a record of marshes drained rather than marshes created. When, under pressure for reduction of taxes, the Congressman looks for a budget to chop, the work of the Biological Survey — highly scientific, long-range in its planning, not easily showing quick returns in assets in money — is a likely victim.

What Congress does is your business and mine. If my Congressman does not understand my interests, that is more than half my fault. If you know of a marsh whose existence is threatened by Federal or State agencies, it is up to you to bring the pressure that will save it. What can one man do alone, you ask? My Congressman tells me one man can do wonders, and that a single sincere letter, which is obviously not prompted by a lobby, means more to him that a petition signed by a thousand names. However, the right organized societies can do a fine job for you too. The Isaac Walton League, for instance, the Audubon Society, the Wilderness Society will take an immediate interest in your problem.

For this too is part of the America we all love — this half-world between land and water, beautifully untamed, unimproved, beyond improvement. It remains a refuge not only for the creatures and the plants that abide there, but for those to whom a few hours of solitude with the wind and water, the reeds and the birds and the shadows of fish, are profits past computing. Let us keep it, then, not only for ourselves but for those sons who, in each generation, are happy there, and there, perhaps, may meet — sportsman and naturalist — on common and cherished ground.

Donald Culross Peattie (1898–1964) was one of the most influential American nature writers of the twentieth century. Peattie was born in Chicago and grew up in the Smoky Mountains of North Carolina, a region that sparked his interest in the immense wonders of nature. He studied at the University of Chicago and Harvard University. After working for the U.S. Department of Agriculture, he decided to pursue a career as a writer. In 1925 he became a nature columnist for the *Washington Star* and went on to pen more than twenty fiction and nonfiction books over the next five decades. Widely acclaimed and popular in his day, Peattie's work has inspired a modern age of nature writing.